# *The East End Plays: Part 2*

# The East End Plays
# Part 2

*Three plays by*

George F. Walker

Talonbooks
1999

Talonbooks
P.O. Box 2076, Vancouver, British Columbia, Canada V6B 3S3
www.talonbooks.com

Typeset in New Baskerville and printed and bound in Canada by Hignell
Printing.

Second Printing: September 2005

The publisher gratefully acknowledges the financial support of the
Canada Council for the Arts; the Government of Canada through the
Book Publishing Industry Development Program; and the Province of
British Columbia through the British Columbia Arts Council for our pub-
lishing activities.

The Canada Council    Le Conseil des Arts
for the Arts          du Canada
since 1957            depuis 1957

Canada

**Canadian Cataloguing in Publication Data**
Walker, George F., 1947-
  The East End plays : part 2

  ISBN 0-88922-404-8
  I. Title.
PS8595.A557E32 1999      C812'.54      C98-910719-1
PR9199.3.W342E32 1999

# CONTENTS

# Introduction

These three plays, premiered between 1987 and 1993, continue George Walker's serio-comic investigation into the possibilities of individual and social transformation in a nameless North American city (probably Canadian, most likely Toronto.) Walker's other East End trilogy—*Criminals in Love, Better Living* and *Escape from Happiness*—uses the microcosm of family to explore the conditions of the relatively powerless. Nora, her daughters and son-in-law initially respond with fatalism to an intimidating patriarchy of criminal fathers. But tentatively and erratically, they make their way towards the genuine prospect of better living.

This second set of East End plays looks at ways of rehumanizing the dehumanized. In *Beautiful City* and *Love and Anger* the city has been given over to the interests and values of criminal developers, wealthy lawyers and tabloid publishers. The architectural ideal is an underground mall that conceals poverty and reinforces "indigenous anxiety." The civilized city has become the social darwinist jungle. Socio-economic issues are subsumed in the dynamics of a single relationship in *Tough!* But there too the question is whether, in responding to his girlfriend's pregnancy, the young man is going to be "an animal" or "a human being."

The thrust of all three plays is the attempt, mostly by women, to re-educate the corrupted and generally bewildered men responsible for the intolerable status quo. The strategy employed by Tina and Jill on Bobby in *Tough!* is to "bludgeon him with accountability," as *Love and Anger*'s Petie Maxwell advises one of his allies. The two women struggle against the inertia of deeply entrenched gender and class conditioning, their own as much as Bobby's. They mercilessly prod him towards a new consciousness, a new sense of his own possibilities in, literally, painfully funny ways. Acting as agents of change, they themselves are subtly but perceptibly changed in the process.

The unlikely catalyst for change in *Love and Anger* is Petie Maxwell, a corporate lawyer born-again in late middle age as a social revolutionary. In his messianic zeal to remake the world he employs questionable tactics and sometimes patronizes the people he wants to help. But Petie does know the enemy: Conner, whose "fascist rag ... panders to everything weak and uncertain and uninformed in the human race," and his toadying lawyer Harris. Together they help maintain a city that, in Connor's words, "has got to be a place for winners." Petie rallies the ostensible losers—the Black woman whose husband has been unjustly imprisoned, the mental patient and her sister—into a motley army of the marginalized. Although their often hilarious bludgeoning fails in the end, the quixotic mission leaves the women energized and empowered. *Love and Anger* obviously affected audiences as well, becoming the longest running non-musical play in Toronto's history.

By far the most successful transformations occur in *Beautiful City*, which has the advantage of a catalytic character who may be a witch. "Fixing the wounded life force," Gina Mae gives to the architect made sick by selling his soul to developers the means of healing himself. She reluctantly reforms her hapless criminal brother-in-law (though she writes off his hopelessly criminal son—after turning him into a crow.) Most impressively, she confronts the big developers and leverages from them enough money for new parks, homeless shelters, low-cost housing, "a throbbing, connecting, living, creative neighbourhood." The heavily armed, extremely unorthodox policewoman who helps her understands that these marvelous events are "a kind of popular fantasy." Perhaps Walker offers this up as a visualization exercise for his audience: you need first to be able to fantasize social reform in order to see it through.

Such provisional reforms as do occur in these plays take place in a rundown old building, a back alley, a park littered with needles. Walker's East End cityscape, while lacking some amenities, is dynamic with the possibilities of renewal. It's the end of town, after all, that first sees the dawn.

**Jerry Wasserman**
*Vancouver, 1999*

# Beautiful City

*Beautiful City* was first produced in Toronto by The Factory Theatre. It opened on September 30, 1987 with the following cast:

**TONY RAFT**  Dean Hawes
**PAUL GALLAGHER**  Benedict Campbell
**MARY RAFT**  Patricia Collins
**JANE SABATINI**  Paulina Gillis
**MICHAEL GALLAGHER**  Hardee T. Lineham
**STEVIE MOORE**  Robert Backstael
**GINA MAE SABATINI**  Deborah Kipp
**DIAN BLACK**  Michelle Fisk
**ROLLY MOORE**  Peter Blais

(Later in the run ROLLY was played by John Dolan.)

Director: Bob White
Set Designer: William Chesney
Lighting Designer: Robert Tomson
Original Score: John Roby

*Persons*
**TONY RAFT**, early forties
**PAUL GALLAGHER**, forty
**MARY RAFT**, early sixties
**JANE SABATINI**, eighteen
**MICHAEL GALLAGHER**, thirty-seven
**STEVIE MOORE**, twenty-five
**GINA MAE SABATINI**, thirty-eight
**DIAN BLACK**, thirty-five
**ROLLY MOORE**, fifty

*Place*

Urban landscape. In the distance mostly glass. The rest is worn concrete, bare—and filled with a minimum of set pieces as required.

*Note*

Intermission should be placed between Scenes Six and Seven.

# Beautiful City

*Late evening.*

*High-rise office. A desk. A working chair. A lounging chair. A model of an apartment on the desk.*

PAUL GALLAGHER *and* TONY RAFT *are staring at the model. Both are wearing suits.* TONY *is immaculate and drinking heavily.* PAUL *is coming undone, sweating, swaying, and not drinking anything.*

**TONY:** This is the future.

**PAUL:** Shit.

**TONY:** What?

**PAUL:** I've got a pain in my side. Could be my appendix.

**TONY:** I want to show you the specs here.

**PAUL:** I've got to go lie down somewhere.

**TONY:** Just hold on a minute. This is for your eyes only. Can you focus in on this. I'm asking you. It's important.

**PAUL:** Make it fast.

**TONY:** Okay. First the big picture. Four thousand square feet. Does it look smaller than that.

**PAUL:** Yes.

**TONY:** It is. We're bending the truth here. Notice the alcove outside the entrance. Four units share the alcove.

**PAUL:** But, you add the size of the alcove to the total size of each unit.

**TONY:** Right.

**PAUL:** God that's pathetic, Tony.

**TONY:** It's an essential lie. Four thousand square feet is the essential minimum. Dumber men than us are selling bigger for less. Okay it's touchy. We'll talk about it later. But look at the layout. Look at the kitchen. It's part of the international series. This one is Japanese. We call it the Samurai. Look at the layout. It screams efficiency. This is a kitchen for people who are deadly serious about their food.

**PAUL:**   Hurry up. I'm going to barf.

**TONY:**   It's the primary living space we're not sure about. That's why you're here, guy.

**PAUL:**   So ... (*groans*) ... what's wrong with it.

**TONY:**   Well it ... just sits there.

**PAUL:**   You want it to move?

**TONY:**   Sure, if you can pull it off. No, look, I'm serious here. Look at it. It's big enough, right?

**PAUL:**   Yeah. I guess so.

**TONY:**   Bright enough too. Remember this is all southern exposure here. So what's the problem. Look at it. Come on get in there with your brain. Feel it. Throw it around. Do it now. This is important.

**PAUL:**   Maybe it's all right. It looks all right.

**TONY:**   Forget the model. Use the concept. I'll give you what I've got. It's in my head.

**PAUL:**   The concept?

**TONY:**   The basic thing. The basic thing is ... you're sitting in the primary living space. Maybe you're a man, maybe you're a woman. Who gives a shit.

**PAUL:**   I've got to sit down.

**TONY:**   Who's stopping you.

> PAUL *sits.*

**TONY:**   Good. Close your eyes ... You're sitting in the model suite  in the primary living space ... and the sales guys have left you alone. You've got a coffee. You've got the brochures. All the bumpf. You've done that stuff, the reading, the talking—now you're alone ... And it comes up into the front part of your brain. A million five. A million five. Is this place worth that much money. Forget the southern exposure, the state of the art security system, the pools, the sauna, the weight room, the diet room, the committee room, the convenience store, the liquor store, the personalized parking space. Forget the Italian tiles in the bathrooms. Forget the fucking bathrooms altogether. All three of them. Forget the Samurai kitchen, the generationally conceived bedrooms, the solarium, the atrium. Forget everything except the primary living space. Because that's the ticket, that's where it happens, that's where you ... live. So ask yourself, are you going to be pleased, are you going to feel good about spending one and one half million dollars on what is essentially four bare eggshell-surfaced goddamned walls?!

> PAUL *groans. Clutches his stomach. Pulls up his knees. Rocks. Falls over onto the floor.*

**PAUL:** Something ... ruptured! You gotta ... get me to a hospital.

**TONY:** First. Answer my question. Come on. This is important.

> PAUL *groans.*

**TONY:** Come on. (*he kneels in front of* PAUL) I've got a dream for this city. It's a beautiful dream. But it's expensive. People have to pay for it. All you have to do is answer my question and I'll get you some help.

**PAUL:** No.

**TONY:** No what?

**PAUL:** No ... wouldn't pay a million five.

**TONY:** Shit ... No. Great. Okay that's honest. Okay I knew that anyway. So ... so you'll fix it. Right?

**PAUL:** Right.

**TONY:** Okay. Stay there.

> TONY *goes to desk. Picks up phone.*

**TONY:** So what was it—two months ago—you said you'd never work for me again. I knew you didn't mean it. (*he pushes a buzzer*) Who's this. Oh hi Mom. Where's Joanna. (*looks at his watch*) So soon? Well could you do me a favour, Mom. Dial 911. Tell them we need an ambulance. No I'm fine. It's Paul. Well I think it's just gas. But he thinks it's his heart.

**PAUL:** Appendix ... No, damn. I had my appendix out fifteen years ago.

**TONY:** So what is it then. Never mind. (*to phone*) Tell them he's been poisoned ... No that's ridiculous. Tell them it's an anxiety attack.

PAUL:   Jesus. It's not anxiety. If you tell them that they won't come.

TONY:   (*to phone*) Tell them it's his heart. (*hangs up*) I wanted to say heart right at the beginning. We could have saved a lot of time. Truth is ... I know it's an anxiety attack. I have that effect on you. It's just one of those chemistry things. Besides ... I know anxiety when I see it. In fact if I don't see it I get a little anxious myself. No seriously take deep breaths. You look better. How do you feel. I think you look better. Do you want me to help you into the chair.

PAUL:   If it's not too much trouble.

    TONY *does.*

TONY:   When I first came to this city one of the first things I noticed was how much anxiety there was around me.

PAUL:   Yeah you have that effect on a lot of people.

TONY:   What? No ... I'm talking about something that was already here. Indigenous anxiety. It runs very deep. You know what I think about that though? I thought this right away. The anxiety here is so deep and so widespread, it's like a natural resource. It can be used. I made a mental note to use it some day. And something else I noticed—maybe this is connected ... I noticed a kind of conspiracy to hide the poverty in this city. So I went looking for it. Found it. Kept it there ... Thought I might use that one day, too. You see I figured that was a characteristic thing about this place— wanting to pretend there were no poor people here. Just people who aren't rich yet ... I mean that's some lie. That's a lie that could be used one day in a major entrepreneurial sociological move. That day is close at hand, guy.

    MARY RAFT *comes in. She is a striking fashionably dressed sixty-year-old woman. Calm forceful expression.*

MARY:   The ambulance is on the way. How is he doing.

TONY:   Great. Aren't you, Paul.

PAUL:   No.

MARY:   He seems to be in genuine pain.

TONY:   I never said he wasn't in pain. But pain's not necessarily a serious thing. Other than the pain, he's great. Aren't you, Paul.

PAUL: No, you asshole. No!

TONY: Calm down, guy. Don't talk like that in front of my mother. She'll think we don't get along.

MARY: Shut up for a moment, Tony. Is there something I can do for you Mr. Gallagher until the ambulance gets here.

PAUL: No.

TONY: Hey where are my manners. Paul, you've never met my mother have you. Tell him what you think of the city, Mom. It's beautiful isn't it.

MARY: I don't believe this is the proper—

TONY: Paul designed a lot of the buildings here. Some of the most dazzling things here came right out of his brain.

MARY: I have to go now. I have a meeting. A meeting about something you should have taken care of a long time ago, Tony. I'm sorry, Mr. Gallagher. I hope it's nothing serious.

TONY: He'll be fine.

MARY: Goodbye.

*She leaves.*

TONY: So whatya think?

PAUL: About … what?

TONY: My mother. I mean I bet you never pictured me with a mother.

PAUL: I did … but she had scales.

TONY: Good for you. You're talking like a real prick. You'll be fine. You want to know why she's here? Actually I'm not sure why she's here. But I think maybe she wants to watch me in action. Get closer to my dream. She never thought I'd amount to much. But everything I am I owe to her.

PAUL: Have you told her that.

TONY: My mother was born in a police state. Eventually she escaped. Married my father. After that she was American. Nothing much. Oh she became part of my father's powerful family. But when she lived in a police state she had values. I got my dream for this city from the part of my mother that's still under siege. It's based on family. Family and safety.

Everything indoors. My motto is "No more strangers in your life." What do you think of it.

PAUL *has passed out.*

TONY:   Paul. Paul? Hey, Paul. Come on. Come on, Paul. Paul. Hey hey, Paul. (*sings*) Hey hey Paul. (*smiles*) Come on. Wake up. Come on, Paul. Hey come on ... Paul, really. Come on, Paul.

*Blackout.*

*Siren.*

## SCENE TWO

*Early evening.*

*A hospital room. One bed.*

JANE SABATINI *is changing the bed. She wears the uniform of a hospital volunteer. She is slim, angular.*

*After a moment,* PAUL GALLAGHER *comes on in a wheel chair. He is wearing a bathrobe over pyjamas.*

**JANE:**  There you are. I thought you got lost.

**PAUL:**  I did.

**JANE:**  You should have waited for an orderly. This is one of the biggest hospitals in the world.

**PAUL:**  It's also one of the worst designed. Nothing seems connected except for those dreadful underground tunnels. And they all seem to lead to the morgue.

**JANE:**  You want me to help you up?

**PAUL:**  I can manage.

*He gets into bed slowly. She is putting the dirty linen in a canvas bag. When she finishes that she begins to arrange his pillows and blankets.*

**JANE:**  Did the x-rays show anything.

**PAUL:**  Why would they tell me. They're my intestines. But the x-rays belong to the doctor.

**JANE:**  Ulcers. That's what everyone says. The nurses, I mean. No one thinks it's cancer … Oh, I'm sorry. I'm not supposed to say cancer. Oh, said it again. Sorry.

**PAUL:**  That's all right.

**JANE:**  No it's on your mind now isn't it. How can it not be. I said it twice. My mother would kill me.

**PAUL:**  Your mother works here?

**JANE:**  No my mother works at Bargain Harold's. But she's really a witch.

**PAUL:**  I'm sorry?

**JANE:**  She's descended from witches. I was one too but she took my power away at birth. My father made her do it. I'm kinda glad. It's awesome. The power is awesome but it kinda removes you from the rest of the world. Puts you in opposition. Like when I told my mother I was doing this work here, she was totally against it. She thinks everyone who works in a hospital does more harm than good.

**PAUL:**   Maybe she's right.

**JANE:**   I try to help.

**PAUL:**   Oh. Yes. I'm sorry. You do.

**JANE:**   You look weird. What's wrong. You in pain?

**PAUL:**   Yes!

**JANE:**   Well don't take it out on me. I do my part the best I can. I know it's not much. A clean bed. A little juice.

**PAUL:**   Yeah. It's great. The juice is great.

**JANE:**   Are you being hostile. I'm sensitive to hostility for some reason.

**PAUL:**   No. I'm—

**JANE:**   Sure. You're a bit hostile. I don't blame you. You're sick. You're entitled. My mother is hostile and she's healthy as a horse. Witches never get sick. Oh they die. But it's like someone just pulls a plug on them. Nothing leads up to it. They're immune to every virus known to science.

**PAUL:**   Listen ... are you being serious.

**JANE:**   Okay okay I know it sounds crazy. But I've seen her in action. She once turned a cat into a raccoon. When I'm telling people about her I just ask them to keep an open mind. No one is smart enough to know everything about life, you know. There are people in this world who are turning things into other things all the time. Listen I shouldn't be telling you this. I mean this is a hospital for God's sake ... But if they can't find out what's wrong with you, maybe you could go see my mother.

**PAUL:**   So that she can turn me into a raccoon.

**JANE:**   Nah. She just did that because she was in a snit. She usually confines herself to better things. She calls it "keeping the power lofty." She cures.

**PAUL:**   So what's that mean exactly. She's some kind of faith-healer?

**JANE:** Actually it has nothing to do with faith. You don't have to believe in shit. No what my mother does for people is teach them how the world really works. The "simple ugly truth," she calls it. She says when they understand they get better.

**PAUL:** Couldn't you just tell me the simple ugly truth and save me a trip.

**JANE:** It's different for each person.

**PAUL:** What's yours.

**JANE:** I'm not supposed to tell. If you press me I will. I'll do just about anything to keep people happy. Oh well there it is, I've just told you.

**PAUL:** Told me what.

**JANE:** My simple ugly truth. Now if you want to know what yours is, I'll tell you how to get in touch with my mother.

MICHAEL GALLAGHER *comes in. He is wearing work clothes. Carrying several large rolls of papers.*

**MICHAEL:** Oh. You look all right. I was scared, boy. I was scared you'd look like death.

**PAUL:** Hi.

**MICHAEL:** Yeah, hi.

**PAUL:** This is my brother. Michael.

**JANE:** Hi. I'm Jane.

**MICHAEL:** Is he all right, really?

**JANE:** I don't know. (*to* PAUL) I'll be back in awhile.

*She leaves.*

**MICHAEL:** Why doesn't she know if you're all right.

**PAUL:** She's a volunteer. She's not a nurse.

**MICHAEL:** So should I go ask a nurse.

**PAUL:** Or you could ask me.

**MICHAEL:** Oh, yeah. Well how—

**PAUL:** I don't know either.

**MICHAEL:** That sounds serious. If they're keeping something from you it could be serious. Don't worry now. I don't want you to worry. But maybe you should get prepared for the worst.

**PAUL:**  Okay.

**MICHAEL:**  I'll come back later.

**PAUL:**  You just got here.

**MICHAEL:**  Yeah but you look tired.

**PAUL:**  I thought you said I looked all right.

**MICHAEL:**  I was lying. You look really bad. What's wrong with you. Oh that's right you don't know.

**PAUL:**  What are those drawings?

**MICHAEL:**  Look. This is business. I shouldn't have brought them. You don't really want to look at them, I know. But …

**PAUL:**  Is it stuff from Tony Raft.

**MICHAEL:**  Yeah.

**PAUL:**  He put me in here you know.

**MICHAEL:**  Really?

**PAUL:**  Well that's what I think. Too many years of listening to his bullshit. It infected my body like a poison. I don't think we should work for him anymore. He's a crook.

**MICHAEL:**  Not technically. Technically he's okay.

**PAUL:**  All right, he's a good crook. He's the best in his field.

**MICHAEL:**  You think all developers are crooks.

**PAUL:**  No I don't. I think Raft is a crook.

**MICHAEL:**  But not technically all right. Let's keep that straight. We need his business.

**PAUL:**  Do we? Do we still need him.

**MICHAEL:**  Oh yeah. No doubt. He's kept us so busy the last ten years we never got a chance to develop new clients.

**PAUL:**  You were supposed to work on that.

**MICHAEL:**  Well I tried. But I was too busy.

**PAUL:**  We could try again.

**MICHAEL:**  Too risky. He's our ticket. I've got a mortgage. I've got kids to educate.

**PAUL:**  I don't.

**MICHAEL:**  Yeah. You've got nothing. You're lucky in a pathetic kind of way.

PAUL: Thanks.

MICHAEL: Listen I'm sorry. But maybe you really should look at these drawings.

PAUL: The condo.

MICHAEL: What?

PAUL: The primary living space needs re-doing. That's the poisonous bullshit he was killing me with last night.

MICHAEL: No. That was a come on. I fixed that for him this morning. He was just screwing you around. He told me he was drunk.

PAUL: I don't get it.

MICHAEL: Well at your last meeting you told him to die and go to hell forever. The condo thing was his way of making friends. You know, just something to get the two of you communicating again.

PAUL: Communicating? You should have heard him. He was raving worse than ever. I think he's finally gone over the edge.

MICHAEL: It's better for us if you believe that technically he was just drunk. And I'll tell you why. Because he's giving us this. (*holds up the drawings*) The big project. The mall.

PAUL: What mall.

MICHAEL: You know, *his* mall. The waterfront extravaganza.

PAUL: Oh Jesus. Not again.

MICHAEL: This time for real. He's got an opening at city hall. He smells a possible go ahead.

PAUL: No way. No way are they going to let him build that monstrosity down there.

MICHAEL: He smells it. He smells things pretty well, Paul.

PAUL: It's Disneyland. No it's worse. It's Lego under glass.

MICHAEL: Not if we design it.

MICHAEL *is unrolling the plans on the bed.*

PAUL: He's already designed it. I've seen it.

MICHAEL: No. He's had a change of mind. He wants us to take his basic notions. And actually do the design. Not just the cosmetics. These are just primitive renderings. We've got carte blanche. Well almost blanche. There are a few grey areas. Things to be negotiated. But aren't there always. I figure the job is worth two million to us.

**PAUL:**  There's a pan under my bed.

**MICHAEL:**  A what.

**PAUL:**  A pan. I'm going to vomit.

**MICHAEL:**  No. Are you serious.

**PAUL:**  Get it.

**MICHAEL:**  I think you're getting carried away here. What's that on your mouth. My God. It's blood.

> PAUL *feels his mouth. Looks at his hand.*

**PAUL:**  Jesus. I'm hemorrhaging.

**MICHAEL:**  Paul. What's wrong with you. Can't you stop that.

**PAUL:**  I'm going to throw up.

**MICHAEL:**  This is serious isn't it. This really is serious. Okay, should I get someone. Yeah. I'll get a ... doctor, or someone like that. Okay. Hold on. (*he runs off*)

**PAUL:**  You, forgot the pan. (*groans*) Oh. Shit. I'm dying here.

> *He leans over the bed. Wretches.*
>
> *Blackout.*

## SCENE THREE

*Near midnight.*

TONY'*s office.* MARY *is sitting at the desk. Going through a set of account books.* TONY *is pacing.*

**TONY:**  He's got some kind of mysterious disease. They've got him quarantined. Do you believe that. The doctor says it's a virus. Never been seen before. Then he says maybe it's not a virus. Maybe it just looks like a virus. It sounds spooky. Maybe we should check ourselves into a private clinic. I can't afford to get sick now. I'm hot. I'm about to succeed beyond anyone's wildest imagination.

**MARY:**  Tony. There's something I've been meaning to ask you … Are you on drugs.

**TONY:**  Mom. Come on. What do you mean. I've got a dream. A vision. I'm hopped-up sure. But I'm doing it from in here. In the gut. I'm hot.

**MARY:**  Just asking.

**TONY:**  I'm hot. But I'm worried. I need Paul Gallagher. He's my point man. He's an award-winning architect. Did I tell you that.

**MARY:**  No.

**TONY:**  They love him at city hall. If he's involved with my mall we get a green light for sure. I need him.

**MARY:**  What about his brother.

**TONY:**  Michael? Michael's good. Yeah he's good I guess. But he's never won an award. I tell you the people in this city love awards. Now if Paul dies maybe we could arrange to have Michael win an award—but all that takes time—

**MARY:**  Tony. These books won't do.

*She closes them.*

**TONY:**  No, they're good books, Mom. They're set up right. Just like Dad taught me.

**MARY:**  Times have changed. Auditors have changed. These books are primitive. The categories are too wide. The time frame—

**TONY:**  Don't make me paranoid about the books, Mom. I don't need that right now.

**MARY:**  I'm telling you. If you're smart you'll listen.

**TONY:**  Okay. I'll bring someone in. Someone new ... That's it! We'll get Paul a new doctor. A genius. He needs a genius.

**MARY:**  Tony. Sit down. We have to talk.

**TONY:**  We're talking.

**MARY:**  Sit down!

TONY *sits.* MARY *stands.*

**MARY:**  I have to tell you something, Tony. We're unhappy.

**TONY:**  We are?

**MARY:**  We ... that is, the family ... the family is concerned about your operation here. We feel ... you're overextended that you've lost focus.

**TONY:**  Oh no I—

**MARY:**  We are worried about your future plans. You seem to have forgotten the basic intention of our family in this area of ... our endeavours ... That is ... to make money. Lots of money. Very fast. ... with very little resistance and therefore very little publicity. The harbourfront mall is an example, perhaps *the* example of something we do not want.

**TONY:**  But Mom, the mall is mine—I invented it—it's unheard of. It'll make history.

**MARY:**  We don't care to make history, Tony. The most interesting history has already been made. Besides, people who make history are complex, confused and basically unhappy. We only care to make money. Quietly. The mall is a dead project!

TONY *stands.*

**TONY:**  Oh no please don't—

**MARY:**  Sit!

TONY *sits.*

**MARY:**  Now on to other business. The real purpose of my visit. (*goes to desk. Picks up phone. Buzzes*) Get in here. (*walks to* TONY) Because you have been so obsessed with certain things, you have failed to notice a problem which has arisen for us here. A kind of subversion in our operation. A low-level mismanagement of our resources. It, of course, must be stopped.

> STEVIE MOORE *comes in. He is a young, wiry, nervous man. Leather jacket. Jeans.*

**MARY:** This is Mr. Moore. You can call him Stevie. Mr. Moore this is my son Tony. Tell him what you told me last night.

**STEVIE:** How much. I mean I told you a lot.

**MARY:** Tell him about the taxi business.

**STEVIE:** Sure. Well there's a—he doesn't seem to be listening.

**MARY:** Tony. Pay attention.

**TONY:** Sorry Mom.

> TONY *lifts his head.*

**STEVIE:** There's a man in the east end who's supposed to be working for you people. He was hired on as a shipper in one of your import export shops. The trade there is porn.

**MARY:** Erotica, Mr. Moore.

**STEVIE:** Yeah, erotica, video, magazines, even some life-size posters. The things is—he's in business for himself now. He's doing this incredible curbside business out of a bunch of taxis. He's got a dozen drivers and a few dispatchers working for him and he's moving a lot of merchandise.

**TONY:** He's stealing the stuff from our warehouse.

**STEVIE:** You got it.

**TONY:** How.

**STEVIE:** He's got his ways. He's a sneaky little bastard.

**TONY:** You know him?

**STEVIE:** Yeah. I know him. He's my dad.

**MARY:** Mr. Moore has, with great personal sacrifice, offered to help us put an end to this activity. You, Tony, will give this matter your full attention. Starting now. You will work with Mr. Moore and come up with a plan to solve this problem expeditiously. Quietly. I'm going to my hotel now. Keep me informed. Goodbye, Mr. Moore. Thank you.

**STEVIE:** You didn't tell him about my money.

**MARY:**   He doesn't pay you. I do. When it's done.

> *She leaves.*

> *Pause.*

**STEVIE:**   Okay. I gotta tell you one thing. I can't waste him. He's my dad, right. I can arrange … a few things for you but it's gotta stop before death. Okay?

**TONY:**   Have you ever wanted a place where you could do all your shopping indoors. Then when you finished shopping have dinner, or even a picnic or a roller coaster ride or a free ceramics lesson … and never get rained on.

> TONY *begins to cry.*

> *Blackout.*

## SCENE FOUR

*Bargain Harold's.*

*The checkout area. A few bins of merchandise behind the cashier's desk.*
PAUL GALLAGHER *is looking through the bins. Picking at things.
Looking closely at others. He is wearing an overcoat buttoned to the
collar. He looks awful.*

GINA MAE SABATINI *is standing by the cash register. Looking at* PAUL
*suspiciously. She is a robust looking woman in her late thirties. She is
wearing a smock and corduroy trousers. Reading glasses on a chain
around her neck. No jewellery. Nothing remotely strange in her
appearance.*

DIAN BLACK *comes on. She is a police detective. She is wearing a
fashionable cloth suit. Carrying a light-weight topcoat over her arm.*

**DIAN:** Hi there.

**GINA MAE:** Hello.

**DIAN:** I'm looking for Mrs. Sabatini.

**GINA MAE:** That's me.

**DIAN:** My name is Dian Black. I'm with the police department.

**GINA MAE:** Yes. But can I see some proof anyway.

**DIAN:** Sure. (*takes out her identification. Holds it up*)

**GINA MAE:** Thank you. I'm supposed to ask. This is not about the
robbery last week. It should be. But it's not.

**DIAN:** No … No I'm looking for Rolly Moore. He's your
brother-in-law, right?

**GINA MAE:** Well my husband is dead. But yeah, I suppose I'm still
sort of related to Rolly.

**DIAN:** Can you tell me where I can find him.

**GINA MAE:** I'm going to be honest with you, Dian. I can. But I
won't.

**DIAN:** This is important, Mrs. Sabatini.

**GINA MAE:** Rolly Moore is a crook. He keeps company with other
crooks. Some of them have very little regard for human life.
If I assist you, one of them might come after me with
malicious intent and I would be forced to alter his genetic
construction.

PAUL *drops a can of cut-rate salmon on the floor. They both look at him.*

**PAUL:** It … It just slipped.

**GINA MAE:** I hope you didn't dent that can. That's good salmon. Priced to give poor people a good taste of the stuff. Limited supply. Check. See if it's dented.

**DIAN:** Your brother-in-law is wanted by the police, Mrs. Sabatini. Mrs. Sabatini?

GINA MAE *is still staring at* PAUL.

**GINA MAE:** (*to* PAUL) You. Sir. Have you tried simple aspirin for your condition. I don't believe in much. But simple aspirin is a genuine miracle drug.

PAUL *smiles. Turns around.*

**DIAN:** Mrs. Sabatini?

**GINA MAE:** Yes, Dian?

**DIAN:** I was saying that Rolly Moore, your brother-in-law, is wanted by the police. You could be in trouble if you impede us.

**GINA MAE:** Well I'm certainly not going to impede you, Dian. I'm just not going to help you.

**DIAN:** Maybe if I told you why he's—

**GINA MAE:** I already know why he's wanted. You're very well dressed for a policewoman, Dian. What part of the force are you with.

**DIAN:** I float.

**GINA MAE:** You're sending out very confusing signals. You talk like a policewoman, you dress like a lawyer and you have the brainwaves of a politician. I can't quite get a handle on—

**DIAN:** Mrs. Sabatini, if you don't cooperate I'm going to have to talk to my supervisors.

**GINA MAE:** Is that a bad thing, Dian. Talking to your supervisors? If it's bad, is it bad for you or for me. I guess what I'm asking is, what does it mean—talking to your supervisors, whoever they are.

**DIAN:** It means I'll probably be back. But next time I'll have to—

**GINA MAE:** Next time you could visit me at my home. Come early and have breakfast. We could get to know each other a bit. You have my address, don't you.

**DIAN:** Yes ... Yes I do.

**GINA MAE:** Well then. Unless there's something else.

**DIAN:** No. No not—

**GINA MAE:** Well then goodbye for now, Dian.

> DIAN BLACK *leaves. Shaking her head.*
>
> *Pause.*

**GINA MAE:** Can I help you, sir.

**PAUL:** Are these work socks really three pairs for two sixty-nine.

**GINA MAE:** If that's what it says.

**PAUL:** Amazing.

> *He brings them to the cash.*

**GINA MAE:** That's all?

**PAUL:** Yes. Oh I'll take one of these pens.

> *He picks one out of a container on her counter.*

**GINA MAE:** Bic pens. The original Bic pen. Not one of those copies. Best buy for your money on the market. All this month you get three for the price of two.

**PAUL:** Oh. Great.

> *He takes two more. She begins to ring the items in.*

**PAUL:** Are you psychic?

**GINA MAE:** What was that sir.

**PAUL:** I couldn't help overhearing. You seemed to know what that policewoman was going to say before she—

**GINA MAE:** She was talking about an habitual personality. In habitual trouble. I know the personality and the trouble real well. No surprises. It's getting harder and harder to get surprised in this life. Have you tried aspirin.

**PAUL:** No.

**GINA MAE:** Actually now that I see you up close I can tell you're beyond the powers of aspirin.

**PAUL:** Really. How sick am I.

**GINA MAE:** Very sick. I have to tell you this. It's my duty in a way. You're probably dying.

**PAUL:** Really? Can you help me.

**GINA MAE:** I have to be careful. You know how it is. I mean are we making a connection here or am I just projecting.

**PAUL:** Your daughter sent me.

**GINA MAE:** Which one. I've got five of them.

**PAUL:** Jane.

**GINA MAE:** Jane's the best. The others all left home. I never see them. And, they're really young. They all got away from me as soon as they hit puberty. If Jane sent you I'll try to help. But it might be hard on you.

**PAUL:** The simple ugly truth.

**GINA MAE:** We'll have to get to know each other. I'll have to pose some questions. Set up experimental situations. See how you respond. But time's a problem. I take my work very seriously.

**PAUL:** Of course. Matters of the spirit—I understand.

**GINA MAE:** I meant my work here. I love this place. You know there are some real and true bargains in this store. People who don't have much money can sort of get by if they shop here. I'm not talking about the really poor, the really poor are screwed no matter what.

**PAUL:** The socks are a terrific bargain. Good work socks are important. You can wear them all year round. You can wear them at home instead of slippers.

**GINA MAE:** We'll get along fine. If I can keep you alive.

*She punches the cash register.*

**PAUL:** Yeah … I'm feeling pretty weak. I've got this pain. It starts over here and then it moves sort of—

**GINA MAE:** That'll be three dollars and forty-nine cents … Do you want a bag?

*Blackout.*

## SCENE FIVE

*An alley. A large mound of green garbage bags.*

*GINA MAE and PAUL. GINA MAE is wearing an old battered fur coat and a toque. PAUL has a similar toque on his head. PAUL is leaning against a wall. GINA MAE is nudging the garbage bags with one of her feet.*

**GINA MAE:** I'd sure like to know what these people are throwing out. One person's garbage is another person's meal.

**PAUL:** This isn't much of a restaurant. I took a look when we passed the window. I'm not sure I'd eat their stuff from a plate let alone a garbage bag.

**GINA MAE:** You'd eat it all right. If you were hungry enough. Who's to say—the way you're going—you might be licking the pavement in a few weeks.

**PAUL:** What makes you say that.

**GINA MAE:** Listen you're an educated man with a lot of money, good connections, a strong support system. But don't you believe any of those things will stop the slide into living hell once you're seriously started. All I'm saying is you could have started.

**PAUL:** I'm sick. I'm not sliding into hell.

**GINA MAE:** Maybe it's the sliding that's making you sick. We'll see. How are you feeling now.

**PAUL:** Fine.

**GINA MAE:** Don't lie. Lying won't help.

**PAUL:** Okay. I feel lousy.

**GINA MAE:** But at least your head is warm. Heat escapes from the head. You need all the heat you can get.

**PAUL:** Then why are you making me wait around this alley.

**GINA MAE:** First things first. A bit of life is going to unfold here in a while. Besides I never said you shouldn't get fresh air. Just keep the head covered. Pull it down over the ears.

*He does.*

**GINA MAE:** Do you like that toque. It looks good on you.

*GINA MAE is now actively looking through the garbage.*

**PAUL:**  Yes. Thanks. How much do I owe you.

**GINA MAE:**  Three fifty-nine. You can pay me later. Twenty percent wool. First wash, in cold water please. Expect a bit of the dye to run. After that, clear sailing. It's from Taiwan. I love the place. Taiwan clothes are the best in the world for practical people with low to moderate incomes.

**PAUL:**  Why are you looking through that garbage.

**GINA MAE:**  Curious. Just like to see what they're throwing out. Truth is, I'd love to go methodically through all the garbage in this city. But you hardly ever get the chance. People see you and they jump to conclusions. Call you names. Make you appointments with social workers. Give me a hand here.

**PAUL:**  I'd rather not.

**GINA MAE:**  Okay. I'll do it alone.

*She rips open a bag.*

**GINA MAE:**  Sure. Look at that. I hope they die without the assistance of pain-killers. Bread. It's all bread. Probably just a bit stale. (*holding a couple of slices*) Want a bite?

**PAUL:**  Ah, no thanks.

**GINA MAE:**  Okay, but if you don't taste it you don't get the purest kind of outrage. You just get it second hand. (*takes a bite*) This stuff is edible! I'm mad as hell!!

**PAUL:**  I thought no one is supposed to know we're here. You're yelling.

**GINA MAE:**  Okay, okay. But these people get paid a visit. Put them on the list ... I've got it in my pocket.

**PAUL:**  What?

*She produces a small pad and pen.*

**GINA MAE:**  The list ... Here. (*hands pad and pen to him*) Put their name and address down and put it near the top. I'll continue the search.

*PAUL is writing. GINA MAE is going through another garbage bag.*

**GINA MAE:**  No surprise. No surprise. Oh here's something I didn't expect.

**PAUL:**  Yeah ... you didn't answer my question before. Are you psychic.

GINA MAE: What's that mean exactly.

PAUL: I'm not sure. Are you … a witch.

GINA MAE: You're not sure what psychic means. But you feel more confident talking about witches, do you.

PAUL: You seem to know about some things in advance. And not know about other things.

GINA MAE: Sometimes the signals are real clear. Sometimes I'm just making informed guesses. Maybe I just have a talent for the obvious.

PAUL: Jane says you turned a cat into a raccoon.

GINA MAE: Maybe the cat did most of the work though.

*Suddenly a car's headlights turn into the alley. Above the headlights the glow of a taxi's light.*

PAUL: Jesus. What's that.

GINA MAE: They're here. Okay, just listen to what gets said. Make a note of anything that strikes you as important. If things get nasty run like hell.

*Car door opens. Closes. Three figures in front of the headlights.*

PAUL: Excuse me, are we in a dangerous situation here.

GINA MAE: Probably.

*The three figures are advancing.*

PAUL: They're coming this way.

GINA MAE: That's the general idea. How are you feeling.

PAUL: What? … Ah. Numb. I'm feeling … numb.

GINA MAE: No pain?

PAUL: No. Nothing. Numb.

GINA MAE: That could be good. That could be a good sign.

*We can make out the three figures.* JANE SABATINI, STEVIE MOORE *and* ROLLY MOORE. ROLLY *is a seedy looking man around fifty. Wearing jeans, a baseball jacket, and old cowboy hat. Carrying a cardboard box.*

GINA MAE: Stop, right there. Are you all right Jane.

JANE: I'm fine, Mom.

**GINA MAE:**  Come to me, dear. You two goofballs stay where you are.

> JANE *walks toward* GINA MAE.

**STEVIE:**  Who are you calling goofballs.

**GINA MAE:**  I'm calling the goofballs goofballs.

> JANE *is now close to* GINA MAE.

**JANE:**  Ah, Mom. Have you been going through this garbage.

**GINA MAE:**  Never mind that. Did they give you a hard time.

**JANE:**  Stevie tried to get tough. I set him straight. Hi Mr. Gallagher. How are you feeling.

**PAUL:**  Numb.

**GINA MAE:**  Go stand next to him, honey. If things get perverse he'll protect you. (*to* PAUL) Won't you.

**PAUL:**  What ... Oh, I'll try my best.

> JANE *goes over next to* PAUL.

**PAUL:**  What's she mean if things get perverse.

**JANE:**  It's just an expression.

**GINA MAE:**  We're dealing here with pure slime. Stay alert ... Okay goofballs. Your turn.

> *The two men advance quickly.*

**STEVIE:**  Now listen you crazy bitch. You keep calling us names and I'll get ugly.

**GINA MAE:**  Shut up, you pitiful asshole.

**ROLLY:**  Why you always insulting the boy, Gina Mae. He never did a thing to you.

**GINA MAE:**  He breathes my air, Rolly. I resent it. Tell him to stop breathing and we'll get along fine.

**ROLLY:**  You wanted us here. We're here.

**STEVIE:**  But do we know why. We don't know shit. The slut wouldn't tell us. We're here on good faith.

**GINA MAE:**  If you call my daughter a slut again I promise you'll wake up tomorrow in a tree eating chestnuts. And it'll seem real natural, if you know what I mean.

**ROLLY:**  She can do it, Stevie. Keep quiet.

**STEVIE:** Ah bullshit.

**ROLLY:** You want to be a squirrel? She's talking about turning you into a goddamn squirrel. So be quiet.

**STEVIE:** Total bullshit.

**ROLLY:** Jesus boy I'll hit you. (*hits him*) I'll hit you again. (*hits him*) I'll kick you too. (*kicks him*)

**STEVIE:** Ah shit Dad, when you say "I'll hit you" you're not supposed to hit me eh. It's supposed to be like a warning.

**ROLLY:** I'm sorry. I was nervous. I'm very nervous in this situation. You can understand that can't you Gina Mae.

**GINA MAE:** Hand over that box.

*He does.*

**GINA MAE:** Here, doll.

JANE *takes it. Opens it.*

**GINA MAE:** Is this your merchandise, Rolly.

**ROLLY:** Yeah. I put in a good sampling, just like Janie told me to.

**GINA MAE:** Well, honey?

**JANE:** Sick stuff. All of it. Some of it's about torture. And a few of these girls look under-age.

**ROLLY:** Appearances are deceiving. They look young but they're really very old. And we're truly careful who we sell the torture stuff to. We only sell it to guys in suits.

**GINA MAE:** Rolly. You're taking my dead husband's family name and dragging it through puke. If your brother was alive he'd break your neck.

**ROLLY:** I'm just doin' business, Gina Mae.

**GINA MAE:** There's plenty of other business you can do. You can always go back to stealing cars.

**JANE:** Mom, don't tell him that.

**GINA MAE:** Whatya expect me to do. Tell him to become a brain surgeon? Car theft is just a major annoyance. Everyone's insured. It's the next best thing to a victimless crime.

**ROLLY:** That's a young man's game. I haven't got the legs anymore.

**GINA MAE:** You're touching me with your poison, Rolly. I've warned you before. Keep your poison really close to you and your kid. Don't let it spread into the human race. Do you remember that warning.

**ROLLY:** I do Gina Mae. It's just that I saw an opening and I felt I had to take it.

**GINA MAE:** Pornography is out, Rolly. No more selling filth to the uninformed. Got it?

**ROLLY:** If you say so.

**STEVIE:** Hey. Come on. Get serious. She says no and you nod like a dog. If we wanna sell this stuff we'll sell it.

**GINA MAE:** He doesn't learn, does he Rolly. He was a mean stupid little boy, and he hasn't learned a precious thing. Of course you didn't help. There's a responsibility in being a parent, Rolly.

**ROLLY:** I try to teach him, Gina Mae. (*whacks* STEVIE *a few times, really fast*)

**GINA MAE:** You should have been sterilized.

**ROLLY:** Maybe you're right.

**STEVIE:** Okay. That's enough. Here's a warning from me. Butt out. We came here outta family courtesy. You had your say. It doesn't mean shit to us. So keep your nose out of our business or I'll have some people burn your house down. I ... a ... awk ... awh ... awk ... (*very bird-like now*) awh! awk! awk!

**GINA MAE:** I changed my mind. I thought he'd make a better crow than a squirrel ...

> STEVIE *pulls a gun. Aims it at* GINA MAE. *Then the gun hand turns. Against his will until it has the gun pointed against his own temple.*

**ROLLY:** Please, Gina Mae. He's my only kid. The only one I've got to look out for me in my old age. Don't do it. I'll talk to him. We'll stop. I promise.

**GINA MAE:** That's all I ask.

> GINA MAE *takes the gun from* STEVIE'*s hand.*

**ROLLY:** Thank you, Gina Mae.

**GINA MAE:** You're welcome ...

> STEVIE *backs away in horror. Then turns and runs off.*

**GINA MAE:** Rolly?

**ROLLY:** Yes Gina Mae.

**GINA MAE:** I've decided to help you change your life. It just occurred to me that it's my duty. I didn't do it before because you repulsed me so much I couldn't stand to be with you. But your slide is out of control. In Biblical terms you're in the clutches of Satan. Realistically, you're just a menace to society. Make the necessary arrangements Rolly. You're moving in with me and Jane.

**ROLLY:** I'm sorry, Gina Mae. I don't understand what you're talking about.

**GINA MAE:** It's simple. I'm going to reconstruct you. Turn you into a decent useful human being.

**ROLLY:** Really? Can you do that.

**GINA MAE:** It'd be easier to turn you into a squirrel, but I've got to try.

**ROLLY:** What about Stevie.

**GINA MAE:** Stevie's beyond help. Stevie lives in a dark hole way beyond the reach of good intentions. Now go make your arrangements, Rolly. Get your clothes. Whatever. Hurry up. I said hurry up!

**ROLLY:** Yes Gina Mae ... Yes Gina Mae ...

> ROLLY *runs off muttering "Yes Gina Mae."*

**GINA MAE:** I might have bitten off more than I can chew.

> *Door slams. Lights back up. Turn. Are gone.*

**GINA MAE:** Are you all right, doll?

**JANE:** Sure, Mom.

**GINA MAE:** How about you, Paul.

**PAUL:** I ... I ... well—

**GINA MAE:** Pain back?

**PAUL:** You ... you said I was going to see some life going on ...pornography ... sleazy little punks with guns ... talking like birds ... changing people into new people ... That's real life?

**GINA MAE:** Sure it is. Where the hell have you been living. This is what goes on!! Get used to it.

PAUL:  I ... I don't want to get used to it.

GINA MAE:  Okay. Then die.

PAUL:  What.

GINA MAE:  Oh good God, man. Stop resisting it. It's as plain as the nose on your face ...

PAUL:  What?

GINA MAE:  The simple ugly truth. There's life right here on earth and you're not part of it!! ... Jane. How do you like our new hats.

JANE:  I like them a lot, Mom.

GINA MAE:  Would you like one. We got them in yesterday. They come in black, blue, and maroon.

JANE:  Get me a blue one.

GINA MAE:  I'll get you a blue one. And a maroon one. I get a discount, remember.

JANE:  Thanks.

GINA MAE:  I love you, doll.

JANE:  I love you too Mom.

> *They hug. Start off.*

> PAUL *watches them leave. Gets up slowly. Starts after them.*

> *Blackout.*

## SCENE SIX

*Early evening.*

*TONY's office. TONY is standing, leaning forward, hands behind his back. Staring at a large Plexiglass model on the desk. It is his mall. The roof is sort of like a misshapen green glass turtle shell. Inside are very brightly coloured little constructions. A roller coaster. A waterfall. Etc. Etc. MICHAEL is pacing. Gesturing. Talking as much to himself as to TONY.*

**MICHAEL:** So he's disappeared. Sucked into the vortex. No one's seen him. None of his friends not that he has many. And of course he lives alone, so who's to check up on him anyway. But he used to make the odd contact with humanity. A bartender. His doorman. So he's disappeared. But it wasn't that hard to do. Pitiful. I'm worried. He could be really sick. Depressed. Floating in the river. Do you have any contacts on the police department.

**TONY:** None that I'll use for something like this ... It's trivial.

**MICHAEL:** Come on. He's my brother.

**TONY:** I had a brother once. He disappeared too. Under suspicious circumstances. I was advised to forget about him. I'm giving you the same advice.

**MICHAEL:** I'll be honest ... I need him. Financially, I mean. I'm worried I can't make it without him.

**TONY:** You're probably right ... You know the last time I saw my brother alive, he and my mom were having a vicious argument ... I really don't want to dwell on this subject.

**MICHAEL:** Do you know how many cars there are in my family. Five. Five cars. And they all have to be replaced every two years. The wife, the kids, they've come to expect it. I'll be honest. I'm terrified of my wife and my kids. They're monsters of consumption.

*TONY looks at MICHAEL for the first time.*

**TONY:** Are you heavily insured. The thing is, never be worth more to them dead than alive. If you're going broke, first thing to do is cancel all your policies.

MICHAEL: I'll keep that in mind. I mean I'm not going down without a fight, you know. I've still got my talent.

TONY: Talent isn't enough. You don't have a reputation.

MICHAEL: Can you get me work.

TONY: Why should I. What have you done for me lately. Did you help me redesign my mall.

MICHAEL: I'll be honest. Your mall can't be redesigned in the way you mean it. It's poorly conceived. I'm sorry. I'm being honest. You have to start from scratch ... I'm sorry I'm being honest.

TONY: Why? Why all of a sudden are you being honest. Your future is on the line here. This is the time you should be licking boots.

MICHAEL: Well ... Well I thought you'd admire me for it. I thought you'd really respect a man for being honest when the chips are down.

TONY: Well you were wrong. This is my dream. You're stepping on my dream. I'll be honest with you now. I want to smack you in the face. I want to pick up that phone and arrange to have you killed ... I'm not sure I won't do it, either.

MICHAEL: Maybe I wasn't really being honest. Maybe I was just being, unimaginative. I mean maybe you're ahead of your time. Maybe I just have to forget all my training, open up my head ... look at the design again.

TONY: Look at it now.

MICHAEL: Okay ... Okay now is good. Yeah. Okay.

*He walks over. Looks at it.*

TONY: Well?

MICHAEL: It works. On some basic level it works. It has ...

TONY: Audacity.

MICHAEL: Yes. And something else ...

TONY: A spirit of adventure.

MICHAEL: Look ... I'm sorry. I have to be honest. I won't be really honest. Just enough to clear my head. And then we can move on ... It's ... it's in incredibly bad taste ... Okay. Wait. I've said it. But my head is opening up here. Bad taste is a starting point. I mean what's bad taste except a reaction to someone else's notion of good taste. Let's think of it that way. Let's build on it ... I can do it. Leave it with me. Give me a month.

**TONY:** Twenty-four hours. I have to move fast.

**MICHAEL:** Pressure. No, that's okay. Pressure can be a good thing. I'll think of it as a test.

MARY RAFT *comes on.*

**MARY:** Oh my God. What's that.

MARY *is pointing at the model.*

**TONY:** Garbage. It's yesterday's news. I'm tossing it out. Michael and I were just talking about how stupid it is. Right?

**MICHAEL:** Oh ... Yes. It's one of the stupidest ugliest things I've seen in my entire—

**TONY:** Yes! So it's garbage. It's on its way to the incinerator. Michael's taking it. Take it, Michael.

**MARY:** Leave it where it is for now ... You're Michael Gallagher aren't you.

**MICHAEL:** Yes. And you're?

**TONY:** My mother.

**MARY:** I have some news about your brother Mr. Gallagher.

**MICHAEL:** Is he all right.

**MARY:** No. No he's not. He's in deep trouble.

*She picks up the phone. Buzzes.*

**MARY:** Get in here.

*She puts the phone down.*

**MARY:** That photograph of your brother you gave to Tony ... I had it copied and distributed to some of our employees ... I was worried, you see. I was behaving like a concerned citizen. Nothing more. Some of our employees cover a lot of ground in their work for us. Your brother was seen.

STEVIE MOORE *comes in.*

**STEVIE:** Okay. I'm in. What do I do now.

MARY:  Shut up. Sit down. In a moment I'll ask you to talk. I'll
  give you instructions in the manner in which you should talk.
  You'll follow them. When you've finished talking you'll shut
  up and sit down again.

STEVIE:  I like you. You make things clear. I like that.

MARY:  Shut up.

> *She points to a chair.* STEVIE *sits.*

MARY:  Now first things first. Michael ... may I call you Michael.

MICHAEL:  Yes.

MARY:  I apologize in advance. I'm about to be brutally frank. I
  made enquiries. I know all about you. You're in debt up to
  your earlobes. (*to* TONY) He owes to a bank, to his
  father-in-law, to a finance company, to a loan shark—

TONY:  A loan shark? Michael that's stupid.

MICHAEL:  It's the monsters of consumption. They drove me
  to it.

MARY:  He owes hundreds of thousands. He can be bought. Buy
  him. Do it now. I need him to help me with his brother.

TONY:  Michael. I'm going to outline a contract for you now. A
  contract which will seal your employment to my family. We
  the employer will secure all your indebtedness and give you a
  salary of ... a hundred thousand a year. You the employee
  will swear an oath of loyalty and secrecy and do whatever we
  ask you to do. Failure to comply with your obligations in this
  contract will result in your immediate death.

MICHAEL:  Really? Oh ... well, I ... don't think I'm ready for this.
  This sounds like pretty heavy stuff. I need some time. What
  do you ... I mean what would you be asking me to do.

TONY:  Details like that are forthcoming only after the swearing
  of the oath.

MICHAEL:  I see. Well I just don't think I'm the kind of—

MARY:  Tony. He doesn't understand. You haven't made it clear
  enough.

TONY:  Michael. Look at me. Come here. Closer. That's it.

> *They are eye to eye.*

**TONY:** I was just being polite. It isn't really a contract. A contract is something you negotiate.

**MICHAEL:** I see.

**TONY:** Do you. Are you looking into my eyes clearly and do you really see.

**MICHAEL:** Yes. Yes I do.

**TONY:** Good. Then let's shake on it.

*They shake.*

**TONY:** Now shake my mother's hand.

*He does.*

**MARY:** Welcome to the family business, Michael.

**STEVIE:** What about the oath.

**MARY:** Shut up! (*to* MICHAEL) We'll assume you've already said the oath silently and clearly to yourself, Michael.

**MICHAEL:** Okay.

**MARY:** (*to* STEVIE) You. Stand up.

**STEVIE:** You bet. (*gets up*)

**MARY:** Tell them the story about your father and what happened in the alley. Nothing more. Not about the drugs in the jockey's saddlebags. Not about the hooker in the alderman's limo. Not about your girlfriend Shirley, God help her. Just the alley and your father. And use none of your filthy language. *None.* Now speak.

**STEVIE:** I'm nervous now. You've made me nervous. Sometimes I just swear. I can't help it. It just comes out. It's my aunt. She's been mucking around in my head. I think she mighta scrambled my—

**MARY:** Get on with it.

**STEVIE:** Okay. Okay. It's … It's … it's this okay. It's my dad. He's heavier into his ripoff than ever. I went to see him like we agreed. I told him "Dad this is a warning. These people want you to stop." I told him I'm just a fuck—fuh—freakin' messenger. He laughs, pats me on the head, tells me not to worry. Says he's getting big. Says you assholes can't touch him. Assholes was *his* word. I'm just telling you. Anyway I say okay, whatever. He's my dad. I'm with him all the way—

**MARY:** Into the alley!

**STEVIE:** Okay. Yeah. We're in the alley. My cousin brought us there. My cousin's a slut. A slut! Slut! Slut! I hate her! Okay I'm sorry. Is slut a bad word really—I'm sorry. We're in the alley to meet my aunt. I don't know why. I ain't gotta clue. I know shit at this point. (*looks at* MARY) But my dad seems scared. Stuff gets talked about. I'm startin' to put the pieces together. My aunt is the brains. She's pulling my dad's strings like he's a dummy without a prick … a dick … A weenie? … Anyway my aunt's got plans. She's going to take over the porn, the hookers, the drugs all the stuff this certain big business is running now—I guess that's you people, eh? I mean I didn't know you had that much going on. I'm impressed. I'm really—fuh-fuh-freakin' impressed.

**TONY:** Just continue.

**STEVIE:** My aunt. She's going to take it over pure and simple. She's got inside info. She's got connections. Then I notice him. Up against a wall. A funny hat on his head. He looks like a wino. But he looks familiar. At first I think he looks like a teacher I once had. Then I remember that teacher's dead. So who is this guy. His face is talking to my brain. My brain knows him. Then I remember the picture your mother gave me. It's him. Okay. For sure it's him. My brain works. Ah man when stuff like this happens I thank God I've got a brain. Okay okay okay. More stuff gets said. The guy in the hat says some things. Some really ugly things about you people. Then he tells me to beat it because he's got some stuff to talk to my dad about … So I do. But I've got the picture. They're the competition. My dad's a prickless dickless dummy and my aunt and the guy in the hat are the big shits. Okay I had a choice then. I coulda gone either way. But I decided. I'm with you guys. And you know why?

**TONY:** Because you're a gutless little pile of vomit.

**MARY:** But his brain works, Tony. It's a little brain, and it works very slowly but it works well enough to comprehend the inevitable. You should be sitting down now, Mr. Moore.

STEVIE *sits.*

**TONY:** Do you believe his story, Mom.

**MARY:** I don't see that it matters. Just the possibility that it's true is enough to require us to take some action ... Michael, did your brother ever talk to you about our family's extended business operations.

**MICHAEL:** No ma'am. Not ... specifically.

**MARY:** But of course you'd both heard rumours.

**MICHAEL:** Yes ma'am, we had.

**MARY:** (*to* TONY) It wouldn't have been too difficult for Paul to obtain information from some of our people. They saw him with you all the time. They could have assumed he was one of your confidantes.

**TONY:** Only the stupid ones, Mom.

**MARY:** But we have a lot of stupid people working for us these days, Tony. Gross pathetic stupidity is everywhere. Right Mr. Moore?

**STEVIE:** I've gotta deal with it every day.

**MARY:** Thank you Mr. Moore. That is all. Wait outside.

STEVIE *stands.*

**STEVIE:** Outside the door? Or outside in the street?

**MARY:** Outside the door will do.

*He leaves.*

**MARY:** Tony. When we've finished with that young man, when he's completely betrayed his father and the rest of his family and helped us destroy them—I want you to have his vocal chords cut. He'll be allowed to live. But silently, please.

**TONY:** How do you want this problem handled, Mom.

**MARY:** Well father to son didn't get us anywhere. Let's try brother to brother next.

**MICHAEL:** Okay. Look. I'll talk to him. If it was Paul that kid was talking about maybe he's just flipped out or something. Maybe he's delirious. I'll try to get him to back off.

**MARY:** Yes. Good. Begin by talking. A resolution by negotiation is always best. However, be prepared to go further. Be prepared to take action if negotiations break down. Tony will describe the action to which I am referring. And I'll leave Stevie Moore behind as a spiritual advisor ... Goodbye for

now. (*she starts off*) And by the way Tony. (*stops*) Make sure
that ridiculous model of yours really does get destroyed. It's
only blurring your vision. I need you to see things perfectly
clearly. Don't make me have to punish you too, Tony.
Understand?

**TONY:**  Sure do, Mom.

**MARY:**  That's a good boy.

>   *She leaves.*

**TONY:**  Okay. Things are complex now. Try to stay with me.
We've got to play it very smart. We'll start with the model.

**MICHAEL:**  I'll take it away and burn it.

**TONY:**  No way. It's my dream. It's my monument. It's the
essential ingredient in this city's radiant future. I'm going
outside the family on this one. That's a very very dangerous
thing to do. But it's important to my internal life. Okay. So
we help Mom. We deal with the threat to our family's
business. But we continue with my mall. I'm going to be
asking a lot of you Michael. Remember your oath?

**MICHAEL:**  Who is that to …? The oath?

**TONY:**  Me.

**MICHAEL:**  Not your mother?

**TONY:**  Her too.

**MICHAEL:**  So just tell me. Am I breaking my oath to her by
helping you with the mall.

**TONY:**  If we're smart it won't matter.

**MICHAEL:**  She scares me. I don't want to upset her.

**TONY:**  Solve the problem with Paul. She'll love you like a son.

**MICHAEL:**  Is that how she loves *you*. Like a son?

**TONY:**  I *am* her son. What kind of question is that. If you're
asking if I'm afraid of her, the answer's yes. But that's
normal. Weren't you afraid of your mother?

**MICHAEL:**  No.

**TONY:**  Well maybe you should have been. Maybe you wouldn't
be in the mess you're in now.

**MICHAEL:**  I seem to be caught. I feel caught. This is new … I've
never felt like this before. Oh sometimes my family makes

me—but I figured I could just disappear if they get really dangerous. I guess there's no way I could just disappear from you people.

**TONY:** No way at all. (*picks up phone*) Joanna, put Mr. Moore on the line for me please. (*pause*) Get in here, asshole. (*puts phone down*) Okay. First things first. We put down the revolt.

STEVIE *comes in.*

**TONY:** Do you know where to reach these people you were talking about.

**STEVIE:** Ah fuck. He's fucking asking me if I know where my own fucking family—

**TONY:** Hey! Hey! Hey!! When we're together only one of us talks like that. Only one of us uses that kind of language. And it isn't you scumbag, so who the fuck is it.

**STEVIE:** It's you.

**TONY:** Right! Have you got a gun.

**STEVIE:** I've got five guns.

**TONY:** (*mocking*) "I've got five guns!" I'm not asking to look at your model airplanes, slim dick. I'm asking you if you're armed.

**STEVIE:** I'm armed. (*takes out a pistol*) Good enough?

TONY *takes out a gun twice the size from a desk drawer.*

**TONY:** It'll have to do … Let's go. My time is money.

*He starts off. Reaches* STEVIE. *Puts his arms around him.*

**TONY:** What's your time, slime.

**STEVIE:** Nothin'. My time is nothin'.

**TONY:** Good boy … Come on Michael.

**MICHAEL:** I'm scared, Tony.

**TONY:** We're all scared, guy. It's a scary business. But we have to keep this city under our control. This city has a radiant future. It needs people who believe in that future to be in charge.

**MICHAEL:** I can't move. I'm paralyzed.

**TONY:** Do me a favour will you, puke face.

**STEVIE:** Yes, sir.

**TONY:** If my friend here doesn't make a move to follow me out the door in two seconds. Blow his head off.

**STEVIE:** Yes, sir.

> TONY *starts off.* STEVIE *raises the gun. Points it at* MICHAEL.

**MICHAEL:** (*takes a step*) Thanks. That helped.

> TONY *goes to* STEVIE. *Puts his arm around him.*

**TONY:** Everything's going to be fine. Little problems have to be fixed so we all have time to dream. Have visions. Do you ever have visions, ass-wipe.

**STEVIE:** All the time, sir.

> *They start off.*

**TONY:** Ah, you fucking liar. I love you. Really I do. You make me feel glad I'm alive and I'm not you. (*to* MICHAEL) You gotta love him for that.

> *They leave.* TONY *with his arm around* STEVIE. MICHAEL *trailing behind.*

> *Blackout.*

> *Intermission.*

*A small bare room in a police station. Just a table and one chair.*

*ROLLY MOORE is sitting in the chair. Drumming his fingers on the table top. A half empty coffee cup in front of him. DIAN BLACK is sitting on the edge of the table. Looking up at the ceiling.*

*A moment passes.*

**ROLLY:** Am I under arrest.

*DIAN BLACK takes her purse from her shoulder. Takes out a pack of gum.*

**ROLLY:** Police stations make me nervous ... I'm pretty nervous now ... If that's what you were wondering ... If that's the purpose of all this ... Okay, it worked ... I mean we've been sitting here for two hours. You haven't said a thing. I've asked you maybe thirty or forty times if I'm under arrest ... you haven't said a word.

**DIAN:** Would you like a piece of sugarless gum.

**ROLLY:** What ... ah ... sure.

*She hands him a piece. Takes one herself. They chew for a while.*

**ROLLY:** So is that all you're going to say.

*Long pause.*

**DIAN:** What else do you want me to say.

**ROLLY:** Well you're supposed to ask me questions. You know, grill me. Or you could answer *my* question. Am I under arrest.

**DIAN:** Actually it would be more interesting if you told me how you feel. Do you feel like you're under arrest.

**ROLLY:** I sure do. But you're supposed to tell me. That's the law. And you're supposed to tell me why.

**DIAN:** But suppose we haven't made up our minds yet.

**ROLLY:** About what? If I'm under arrest?

**DIAN:** Or why. Or maybe there are a number of things we haven't made up our minds about. We're faced with a richness of possibilities here.

ROLLY:  Whatya mean. I mean it's good that you're talking. But whatya talking about. You're not talking like a cop. You're talking weird. Go get me a cop who talks like a cop.

DIAN:  They're all dead.

ROLLY:  What?

DIAN:  All the cops who talk like cops. They died.

ROLLY:  Okay let's stop talking for awhile.

DIAN:  Fine.

*Long pause.*

ROLLY:  You're making me real nervous, lady. If I get much more nervous, I won't be any good to you. I'll have a seizure or something. I'm older than I look.

DIAN:  How old do you think you look. That's always an interesting question. Answer that one.

ROLLY:  Hey are you one of those rogue cops. Are you outta control. Are you working without supervision.

DIAN:  I have a supervisor. He talks like me. He taught me everything I know. How old do you think I look. I could go get my supervisor. You could tell me how old you think he looks.

ROLLY:  You're talking like a person who's got no reason to be in a hurry. Those kinda people make me nervous. They've got lots of time to plan their alibis. Okay I'm nervous on a whole new level now. I hope you're happy. Did you put drugs in my coffee. Are you waiting for the drugs to work.

DIAN:  Let me tell you something about myself.

ROLLY:  I'm expected somewhere, you know. People will be getting suspicious. If this is some kind of vigilante thing, if this is magnum force ... I'm telling you it won't work. If you kill me and drop my body in an alley, suspicions will be aroused ... Everyone knows I'm just a petty thief. I've never done anything to deserve that kind of treatment. They'll rule out the mob. You'll be investigated.

DIAN:  I'm single. I'm thirty-five years old. I have a degree in sociology. I'm not afraid of death.

ROLLY:  Why'd you say that.

DIAN:  It's true. All of it.

**ROLLY:** The last part. Why'd you tell me you weren't afraid of death.

**DIAN:** I thought you might want to know. You were talking about it. It was on your mind. It was on both our minds, I guess. In sociological terms, that's called "shared concern."

**ROLLY:** Look. Whose death are we talking about here.

**DIAN:** Whose do you think.

**ROLLY:** Look. I told you. You won't get away with it. I think you're bluffing anyway. I know cops. They bluff. Why the hell won't you tell me what it is you want to know.

**DIAN:** It would be more interesting if you figured out what it is you want to tell us.

**ROLLY:** Yeah?

**DIAN:** In the meantime ... You said you know cops—I find that interesting. Listen when was the last time you had any contact with them.

**ROLLY:** Them? The family?

**DIAN:** No. Cops ... What family. Yours?

**ROLLY:** I'm confused. I'm drugged, right? You're not really talking weird. I'm just hearing weird.

**DIAN:** As for cops. Well times have changed. Methods have changed to keep up with the times. Not being afraid of death is now the basic requirement.

**ROLLY:** That's a threat for sure. I may be drugged but I'm not stupid. Okay. Okay you want to know about the family. I'll tell you.

**DIAN:** You can tell me anything you want. There'd be no problem with that. I don't think it would conflict with the basic requirement.

**ROLLY:** Okay I'm gonna make a wild guess about what you're talking about here. Am I doomed. No matter what I say, am I doomed.

**DIAN:** Do you feel doomed.

**ROLLY:** Yeah. I kinda do. And I'll tell you something.

**DIAN:** Tell me anything you want.

ROLLY:  I don't want to die ... I've got a chance for
rehabilitation. My sister-in-law is a witch. She's going to
remake my personality. In a month or so I could be a useful
citizen. It's true. I was really looking forward to it. I was on
my way to her house when you nabbed me.

DIAN:  You mentioned the mob earlier. I meant to tell you I
found that interesting.

ROLLY:  I could talk about the mob. I could do that.

DIAN:  Then after that, there was some confusion about a family.
I might be interested in some clarification on that ... Would
you like me to put some more drugs in your coffee first.

ROLLY:  You put drugs in my coffee?

DIAN:  I thought you knew. You said you knew.

ROLLY:  Are they dangerous.

DIAN:  One of them.

ROLLY:  One of them? Jesus. How many kinds did you put in.
Jesus am I gonna die. How much of that drug can a guy take
before he dies.

DIAN:  I'm not sure. Do you want to find out. It could be
interesting. Come on. Let's go for it. (*she picks up the coffee
cup*)

ROLLY:  What the hell is wrong with you lady. Give me back that
cup. (*grabs it*) You've weirded me right out. You're weirding
me right to death. Jesus. Get me help. Get me someone to
talk to I can understand.

DIAN:  I could do that. But it wouldn't solve the time problem.

ROLLY:  What's the time problem.

DIAN:  The dangerous drug in your coffee. It takes some time to
kill. That gives us some time to stop it, I guess.

ROLLY:  You really can't get away with this.

DIAN:  I really can. And for one basic reason. Because out of all
the people I know, and all the people you know, there's no
one who gives a shit about what happens to you.

ROLLY:  Jesus. That's the only thing you've said to me so far that
makes any sense. And it was really crappy. Totally depressing.
I think you might not be human. In my drugged and

weirded-out mind I'm seeing you as a space monster. I gotta tell you that. But I'm dying aren't I. I'm delirious ...
Oh Jesus.

DIAN: Offer me some clarification about the mob and about that family you mentioned. That is, if you really want to.

ROLLY: If I do, will you save me.

DIAN: I think there's still time.

ROLLY: Really?

DIAN: There's a chance. Go for it.

ROLLY: God bless you. God bless you!

DIAN: Go for your chance. Make it interesting.

ROLLY: I want to live. I want to be a new person! I want to offer you clarification! I do! Really!

DIAN: Go for it! Come on! Go for it!!

ROLLY: Okay! I know plenty! There's a really big family with really big—

DIAN: Wait. Hold that thought. I have to get a stenographer.

*She leaves.* ROLLY *looks around. Nervously. Looks in coffee cup.*

ROLLY: (*shouting off*) Come on. Hurry up. Hurry up for chrissake! I'm running out of time here!!

*Blackout.*

## SCENE EIGHT

*A small area in a corner of* GINA MAE*'s old house.*

*Two old armchairs.* PAUL *is sitting in one of the chairs. A bowl of fruit on his lap. Eating a banana.* GINA MAE *is sitting in the other chair.* JANE *is sitting on the floor between her mother's legs.* GINA MAE *is playing absentmindedly with* JANE*'s hair.*

**PAUL:** So it's nice here. Your house is comfortable.

**GINA MAE:** Thanks. Eat your banana.

**PAUL:** This is my third. I'm usually not too keen on bananas.

**JANE:** They contain potassium. Maybe you have a potassium shortage.

**GINA MAE:** The thing about bananas is—they're comforting. They're a relaxing food to eat. Because of the texture. Because you have to eat them slow. If you eat them fast you could gag and choke to death. I noticed you ate your first banana real fast … You're lucky you're still alive. When you finish your banana eat an orange. There're seedless clementines. You buy them by the box. Five ninety-nine if you shop around. I recommend them.

**JANE:** Vitamin C.

**GINA MAE:** The colour. The colour and the cool feeling of the juice combine for a positive experience.

**PAUL:** The grapes look good.

**GINA MAE:** Save the grapes. Grapes are for when you need to feel aggressive.

**PAUL:** Are you a vegetarian.

**GINA MAE:** No.

**PAUL:** I thought you know … because of your spiritual beliefs …

**GINA MAE:** You keep referring to my spiritual beliefs. I think you're confusing me with someone else. Maybe one of those mother earth types. I don't have much in common with them. Truth is, I don't have much in common with anyone. I'm an original. When you've come to terms with my originality you'll be on the road to recovery. But back to your question. I eat meat all the time. I have no problems with that. Animals are here to provide meat for other animals.

That's their purpose. You take away that purpose and you leave them with a sorry existence. I know. I've made mental contact with cows. Talk about depressing. If I told you what a cow thought about on a moment to moment basis you wouldn't get out of bed for a week. You'd probably try to commit suicide.

PAUL:   I've been thinking a lot about suicide.

GINA MAE:   I'm glad you brought that up. Of course I provided the opportunity, but I'm glad you took it. Eat an orange.

PAUL:   Okay.

GINA MAE:   Tell me a couple of things about yourself. Have you ever been married.

PAUL:   No.

JANE:   In love?

PAUL:   I was in love once with someone I wanted to marry. She left me because I was more in love with my work. That's what she said. I think she really left me because she realized my work was the only interesting thing about me.

GINA MAE:   Tell me more about your work.

JANE:   An architect is a tremendous thing to be.

GINA MAE:   Does he look like he feels tremendous. Be more specific with your enthusiasm, Jane. Always put time, place and circumstance together. Almost certainly he'd feel tremendous if this were ancient Greece.

PAUL:   Well my work was my life. And I've come to hate it. I've come to hate all the people who derive any use out of my work ... I build places where people can live. I hate the people who live there. I don't know why. I've met them. They're not evil. I don't like the way they dress, but that can't be it. I kept thinking if I could figure out why I hated them I could start building them better places to live. I was working on it when I got sick.

JANE:   When you get really successful you get depressed sometimes. I read an article at the hospital. It's called "attainment of goal depression."

PAUL:  I used to get that every time I finished a project. This is
something else. Bigger. Worse. You know ... maybe we
shouldn't rule out a disease. No offence, but maybe I really
should be going to other doctors.

GINA MAE:  I'm not against that. If you're still alive, in say a week,
but you're not feeling better, go see a doctor. In the
meantime let's talk about money.

PAUL:  Money?

GINA MAE:  Yeah. How much you got?

PAUL:  On me?

GINA MAE:  On you. In the bank. In investments. The whole
picture.

PAUL:  I don't know. My condo is worth about four hundred
thousand, then in the bank, all the rest ... maybe a total of
three-quarters of a million.

JANE:  That's amazing.

GINA MAE:  How the hell did you wind up with that much money.
Were you born into it.

PAUL:  My father was a mechanic ...  I just worked for it. Anyway
it's not that much really.

GINA MAE:  I'm glad you feel that way. Give it all to me.

PAUL:  If you need some money I'd be glad to help out. We
could think of it as payment for helping me, letting me stay
here—

GINA MAE:  Yeah. Sure. Think of it any way you want. And keep a
little to live on. But I want all the rest. Make the
arrangements tomorrow. Put your property on the market.
Visit your bank. Visit your stock broker. Make the
arrangements. I'll help you if you want. So will Jane.

JANE:  Please Mom. You're embarrassing him. He thinks you're
serious.

GINA MAE:  Well he has all that money and it's doing him no
good. Why not get rid of it. See if that helps.

PAUL:  If I gave it to you, what would you do with it.

GINA MAE:  Spread it around in some places where it could be
used. You could help me. So you'll make the arrangements?

**PAUL:** I'll think about it …

**JANE:** You will?

**PAUL:** Yeah. I'm not making any promises.

**GINA MAE:** Neither am I. I'm just giving you an option.

*A knock on the door.*

**JANE:** I'll get it.

*She leaves.*

**PAUL:** So basically you're a do-gooder, right.

**GINA MAE:** Basically so are you. I mean you're a human being. Basically human beings want to do good. You have to believe that. Even if it makes you feel a little stupid. I mean what's the alternative. I'll tell you. The alternative is ugly.

JANE *comes in.*

**JANE:** He's got a visitor.

MICHAEL *comes in.*

**MICHAEL:** Hi … Oh man, you look awful. What's happening to you. You're looking worse every time I see you.

**PAUL:** Oh, well actually I feel a bit better since I got out of the hospital.

**MICHAEL:** You're kidding yourself. You need help. Let's go.

**PAUL:** Thanks anyway. I think I'll stay here for awhile.

**MICHAEL:** No you can't do that. You don't understand.

**GINA MAE:** Excuse me. We haven't been introduced.

**PAUL:** Michael is my brother. Michael this is Mrs. Sabatini. She's—

**MICHAEL:** I know what she is. How the hell did you ever get mixed up with her. Don't you know who you people are messing with. She's got you toying with death.

**PAUL:** Michael. What are you doing here. And what the hell are you talking about.

**MICHAEL:** I cut a deal. You come with me right now, you sever your connection with these crooks and you'll be forgiven—

**JANE:** Who are you calling crooks, mister.

**MICHAEL:**  Look Paul, we haven't got any more time. I have to get you out of here right now.

**PAUL:**  Why?

**MICHAEL:**  (*looks at his watch*) Something awful's going to happen.

**GINA MAE:**  He's right. I can feel it.

**PAUL:**  (*stands*) Whatya mean something awful?

**MICHAEL:**  It's not my fault. The monsters of consumption made me vulnerable.

STEVIE *bursts in.*

**STEVIE:**  Okay. The clock's running assholes. (*to* MICHAEL) Didn't you tell them.

**MICHAEL:**  You told me not to tell them.

**STEVIE:**  I told you not to tell them until it was time to tell them.

**MICHAEL:**  How the hell was I supposed to know when it was time to tell them.

**STEVIE:**  Well you better tell them now. Unless you want part of a murder rap.

**GINA MAE:**  Are you behind this Stevie.

**STEVIE:**  The cops have got my dad. You turned him in, I know you did. And now I'm on a rampage. I told you not to mess with me. You're lucky I feel a duty to warn you. (*to* MICHAEL) Tell them for chrissake!

**MICHAEL:**  It's going to blow up! They've wired the whole house with explosives!

**STEVIE:**  Okay, assholes. You're warned. Fair's fair. I warned you cause you're family. I did my duty. (*runs out*) Assholes. Sluts. Dummies.

*He is gone.*

**PAUL:**  Michael, what the hell are you doing blowing up people's houses.

**MICHAEL:**  What are you doing pushing drugs and selling pornography. I don't know, maybe it's genetic. Maybe there's an ugly criminal gene in the family that's been lying dormant for centuries.

**PAUL:**  This is a mistake.

**MICHAEL:** Tell that to Tony Raft's mother.

**PAUL:** What's she got to do with it.

**MICHAEL:** I swore an oath. I'm gonna be like a son to her. Do you realize what that means. I'm scared shitless.

*GINA MAE is pacing madly. Humming loudly.*

**GINA MAE:** Paul, take Jane and get out of the house.

**PAUL:** Sure. As soon as I find out why this is happening.

**MICHAEL:** There's no time. There's only twenty seconds left … Holy shit. Twenty seconds.

*MICHAEL is squirming. His feet are stationary but his legs are moving up and down.*

**JANE:** Can't you stop it, Mom.

**GINA MAE:** Too late. Get going, Paul.

*PAUL is trying to drag JANE off.*

**MICHAEL:** Holy shit. My feet won't move. (*looks at his watch*) We've got less than twenty seconds and my feet won't move!

**GINA MAE:** This is ugly. This is the ugly alternative. I want my daughter out of here!

*PAUL is pulling JANE out.*

**JANE:** You too, Mom! Please! Please Mom! You too!

**PAUL:** Come on, Gina Mae.

**JANE:** Oh please Mom!

**GINA MAE:** Get her out of here!

*PAUL throws JANE over his shoulder. Leaves.*

**MICHAEL:** Paul. Wait. Come back. I can't move. Someone has to help me move.

*GINA MAE kicks him in the ass, knocking him forward.*

**MICHAEL:** Thanks. (*runs out*)

**GINA MAE:** I was born here. This was my mother's house. My grandmother's house. People who destroy this house are going to have to pay.

*She looks around. Touches some of the furniture affectionately.*

*Blackout.*

*Explosion.*

## SCENE NINE

*Mid-evening.*

TONY's *office.* MARY *is sitting behind the desk. A light meal in front of her.* DIAN *is leaning on the side of the desk. Pounding it with an open hand.*

DIAN: Now listen, lady. I've warned you! Don't try to intimidate me with that tone of voice. And don't make any more threats. Because if you do I'll reach over and haul your satin ass right down to headquarters!! You're talking to the police here! You can't threaten my life. You're operating in foreign territory lady. You're operating on very thin ice!!

MARY: I don't like having my supper interrupted. And I don't like being visited by the police at any time.

DIAN: Tough shit!

MARY: (*stands*) No one talks to me like that!

DIAN: Shut up! Sit down! Put some food in your mouth. And listen!

MARY *sits. Takes a bite of a roll.*

DIAN: I'm here to tell you something. I'm here to give you a message from high up. You were allowed into this city on a number of strict conditions. Your family was allowed to bring your money here and build condominiums and apartment buildings. You were clearly instructed to leave all your other interests where you came from. You were under very strict guidelines. Guidelines that were put in place to guarantee that your "subsidiary" filth would not rear its ugly head in this city. We have very convincing evidence that you have not adhered to these guidelines and I am here to put you on notice. Clean it up. Clean up your mess or get out. My instructions come from the top here and the people I work for have no intention of letting some public gangland bullshit lead to public revelations tying the money that constructed those buildings to a bunch of drug-trafficking porn-trafficking, gambling, pimping hoods ... Well that's it. You got it? I said, have you got it?!

MARY: Yes.

**DIAN:** Great! … I've got to get going. I'm late for my aerobics class.

*DIAN picks up a nylon gym bag from the chair. Throws it over her shoulder.*

**DIAN:** See ya.

*She leaves.*

*Pause.*

*MARY stands. Suddenly. Knocking over her chair. Begins to pace. Suddenly stops. Looks around. Walks over. Picks up her chair. Sits down. Begins to eat.* PAUL *comes in from the opposite direction that* DIAN *left. He is holding* STEVIE *by the collar of his jacket. They are both lightly covered in soot.* PAUL *is carrying* STEVIE's *gun.*

**PAUL:** I've got a message for you. It concerns your son. We've got him. If you want him back you'll have to pay.

**MARY:** How much.

**PAUL:** A lot. We'll let you know. My first instinct was to go to the police. But a wiser mind prevailed. She's got a better plan. You're part of it. You'll be told what it is.

**MARY:** When.

**PAUL:** When we're ready. You people are insane. Insane and stupid. You've made some colossal mistake in identities which is pure stupidity. You make me sick. You make me so sick you're making me healthy again.

**MARY:** Why don't you just calm down and tell me what happened.

**PAUL:** You know. And if you don't know, this piece of sewage will fill you in. Stay by the phone. We're serious. We're mad. And we're heavily armed.

*PAUL throws* STEVIE *across the desk.* STEVIE *lands in the middle of* MARY's *supper.* PAUL *leaves.*

*Pause.*

**STEVIE:** Things turned a little sour. Things got kinda screwed up.

**MARY:** Get off the desk.

**STEVIE:** Okay. But I'm telling ya—

**MARY:** Get off the desk!!

**STEVIE:**   Okay okay. (*he does*) But I'm telling ya that guy's dead in the water. He's dead and just waitin' to get buried. I'm mad. God I'm mad. No one's ever seen me mad. It's terrifying. He's gonna get terrified right to fucking death. Jesus he threw me around like a sack of friggin' onions. Jesus! Sorry about all the bad words. I know you don't like them.

**MARY:**   What did he mean when he said we'd made a mistake in identities.

**STEVIE:**   He's squirming. He might look like he's in control. But we've got him squirming.

**MARY:**   I see. There's no chance that you've lead us astray here.

**STEVIE:**   I don't see how. I was just reporting the things these eyes saw.

**MARY:**   And you *saw* him and your aunt trying to take over our street business. You're still sure of that are you. You didn't construct the whole thing did you.

**STEVIE:**   What? You think I'm lying? Why would I lie.

**MARY:**   To impress us.

**STEVIE:**   Ah shit. Sorry. But ah shit. I've never impressed anyone in my whole life. Why would I think I could start now. I was just trying to save my dad before he got outta control.

**MARY:**   Well it doesn't matter now does it. They have Tony.

**STEVIE:**   Yeah that's weird. How that happened is really weird. We blew the place to bits—

**MARY:**   You did what.

**STEVIE:**   My aunt's house. We blew it to bits. It went up like a goddamn atom bomb. I was with Michael. We started to run. We came around a corner and met up with your son standing by the car. He was still holding the detonator. Like he was in a freakin' daze. We tell him to drop it and get in the car. No answer. We yell at him. You know cause all hell's goin' to break loose. We're yelling, "Come on, come on." He's just standin' in a freakin' daze. Finally he looks at us and says "I can't go. She wants me to stay. I have to make amends." He says he's gotta make amends. That's what he says … So Michael jumps into the car to take off. I'm about to jump in too when I feel a hand on my shoulder then a terrific whack on my head. I wake up and our friend in the hat has me on the ground behind this building with his foot on my face. That's all I know. You know the rest. The rest is what he told you.

*MARY stands. She looks furious. Walks to STEVIE.*

**MARY:**  Whose idea was it to blow up the house.

**STEVIE:**  Ah ... Mine?

**MARY:**  I see. And my son went along with it, did he.

**STEVIE:**  Well I'll tell you the truth, he didn't seem to care. All the way over there he was talking about this enormous shopping mall he wants to build. By the time we reached my aunt's house he was like almost hysterical talking about it. Almost crying, talking about it. Well I knew you wanted us to take some action here so I stepped in. I made the arrangements. He didn't seem to care. I had to take charge. You see, I'm the kinda man who ah, who—ah—

*She has interrupted him by slowly inserting her fist in his mouth.*

**MARY:**  I see. Would you wait outside Mr. Moore.

*She removes her fist from his mouth.*

**STEVIE:**  Ah ... Outside the door? Or outside in the street.

**MARY:**  Just leave.

**STEVIE:**  Sure.

*He does.*

*MARY calmly walks to the desk. Then in a fury sweeps the mess from the desk.*

**MARY:**  Jesus. Fucking! Christ!!

*Blackout.*

*Late night.*

*The same alley as before.* GINA MAE, JANE, *and* TONY. TONY *is sitting on the garbage bags. His hands tied behind his back.*

**TONY:** Poor people live around here don't they. This is one of those areas that are never talked about.

**GINA MAE:** We talk about it.

**JANE:** We live here.

**GINA MAE:** We used to. Someone blew up our house.

**TONY:** I'm sorry about that. I'd like to make it up to you.

**GINA MAE:** You will.

**TONY:** Like I told you, we were given bad information. Your nephew said you were trying to take over.

**GINA MAE:** Never refer to that creature as my nephew. If you do I'll come visit you in your brain again.

**TONY:** Hey. Was that you in there before.

**GINA MAE:** Yes.

**TONY:** That was strange. We had a nice long talk didn't we. But it was strange.

**GINA MAE:** You didn't mind?

**TONY:** I liked it.

**GINA MAE:** Most people can't stand it when I do that.

**TONY:** No no I liked it. You set me straight about a few things. Especially the part about making amends. You see, I think a part of me is really into making amends. I think that's what my mall is really about.

**JANE:** We don't want to hear any more about your mall. It sounds stupid.

**TONY:** Really? Maybe I didn't describe it properly.

**GINA MAE:** It's not needed—we don't need it. If you want to build something that's needed build a huge Bargain Harold's.

**TONY:** Who's he.

**GINA MAE:** I don't know. I don't even know if Harold still exists. But his dream lives on.

**TONY:** Great. I'm attuned to dreams. Maybe me and this guy Harold could team up.

**GINA MAE:** How much money could your mother have come up with in twenty-four hours. Honestly.

**TONY:** Hard to say. Seven or eight million.

**GINA MAE:** Damn. I only asked for five.

**TONY:** Five is no sweat. You'll get that for sure. What are you going to do with it. Travel?

**JANE:** My mom hates to travel. My mom can travel in her brain if she has to.

**TONY:** That true?

**GINA MAE:** I'm not saying.

**TONY:** (*to* JANE) How about you.

**JANE:** I like it here. I like my job. I used to like my house.

**TONY:** Buy a new one. Five million gets you a great house. Or better still buy a condo.

**GINA MAE:** Yuk.

**JANE:** We hate those things. Living in those things is like living away from … you know … life.

**TONY:** That's what's so great about them. Life sucks. People shouldn't have to go anywhere near it. I've got this plan. Tunnels. I'm going to connect all the major downtown living areas by tunnels. Then I'll issue keys to these tunnels so people can visit their friends. But they don't have to meet a lot of strangers on the way. Because everyone in the tunnel will have a key. And the key will mean they have something in common which is that no one in the tunnel wants to have anything to do with anyone else in the tunnel.

**GINA MAE:** You're not an evil man, Tony. You're just not completely human.

**TONY:** Thanks.

> PAUL *rushes on from the end of the alley.*

**PAUL:** Okay. They're coming. Are you ready?

**GINA MAE:** I don't know. Whatya mean by "ready."

**PAUL:**   Prepared. Focussed. Never mind. You'll do fine. I have total faith in you.

*He smiles widely. Puts his hand gently on* GINA MAE*'s cheek.*

**GINA MAE:**   Yeah … thanks … Now go stand next to Mr. Raft. Put the pistol to his head.

*PAUL obeys.* GINA MAE *gestures for* JANE *to come over.*

**GINA MAE:**   (*whispering*) Did you see what he just did. Did you notice the gooey smile he gave me. Did it have a meaning. Just who exactly does he think I am.

*JANE shrugs.* GINA MAE *and* JANE *turn. Look at* PAUL *who is holding the gun to* TONY*'s temple.*

**TONY:**   That thing loaded, Paul?

**PAUL:**   Yes.

**TONY:**   It's just the chemistry between us, isn't it, Paul. Our chemistry just turned bad somehow.

**PAUL:**   You were killing me.

**TONY:**   Nah. I was just giving you honest work.

**GINA MAE:**   Jane, are you nervous.

**JANE:**   It's for a good cause.

**GINA MAE:**   Stand behind me.

**JANE:**   I'd rather you stood behind me, Mom.

**GINA MAE:**   I know you would, doll. But come, get behind me anyway. Just to humour me.

**JANE:**   Okay.

*She does.*

*Pause.*

*Footsteps.* MARY *and* STEVIE *appear out of the shadows. Advance.* MARY *is wearing an expensive, luxurious fur coat.* STEVIE *is carrying two suitcases. They stop in front of* GINA MAE.

**GINA MAE:**   Welcome to our little home away from home.

**MARY:**   Are you all right, Tony.

**TONY:**   Terrific. Take a good look around, Mom. This is one of those poor people neighbourhoods. If we're smart we'll use it one day.

**PAUL:**  You've been using it for years.

**TONY:**  I mean in a positive way. Mom, I've been thinking. I think it's time to start acting positively. It could be a coming trend.

**MARY:**  Be quiet for a moment, Tony. (*to* GINA MAE) You wanted us here. We followed your instructions. The money is in those suitcases. (*to* STEVIE) Show them.

> STEVIE *begins opening up the suitcases.*

**GINA MAE:**  That's a really great coat. Is it real.

**MARY:**  Yes, of course.

**GINA MAE:**  Can I have it. I want to give it to my daughter.

**JANE:**  I don't like coats like that, Mom.

**GINA MAE:**  I feel it's the least they can do for you after destroying your house.

**JANE:**  I'd never wear it. I'd feel stupid.

**GINA MAE:**  (*to* MARY) She doesn't want it. You can keep it.

**STEVIE:**  Holy shit. Look at all this money. Is this real.

**MARY:**  Yes. Of course … Shut up.

**STEVIE:**  Holy shit.

**MARY:**  All right. There's the money. Take it. Turn my son loose. We've finished doing business.

**GINA MAE:**  The truth is we've just started. There's a little problem with the life force that has to be reckoned with here.

**MARY:**  The what?

**GINA MAE:**  You've injured the life force in my neighbourhood. It's going to cost a lot of money to make it better.

**MARY:**  You talk like an insane person.

**GINA MAE:**  Be gentle now. Insane people are ill. Don't annoy me by showing disrespect for genuine illness.

**MARY:**  There's your money. Take it, turn my son loose, let us go about our business. And I'll take no further action against you. Push me and I'll have you and everyone you know obliterated from the face of the earth.

**GINA MAE:**  Now there's an example of what I mean. I'm afraid you have a long way to go in order to get on good terms with the life force. This five million is just a down payment. But as down payments go it's not bad. Stevie. Bring the money over here.

**STEVIE:**  What? (*he is staring at the money*)

**GINA MAE:**  Bring it here!

**STEVIE:**  What?

**MARY:**  Take her the money!

**STEVIE:**  What? … No. I don't think I can. Yeah. That's right. I can't. Look at it. It's right here. It's millions of dollars. I can see it. It's right here.

**GINA MAE:**  Be careful now, Stevie.

**STEVIE:**  It's right here. I'm touching it.

**MARY:**  Be very careful.

**STEVIE:**  No, no. I gotta say it. I gotta have it. I'm gonna do it. Jesus Jesus, I'm gonna—

**GINA MAE:**  Careful.

**STEVIE:**  Ahhhhhh!

**GINA MAE:**  Too late.

> *He pulls out a gun.*

**STEVIE:**  Fuck you. Fuck you all. This is my chance. I see it. Who knows if I'll ever see it again so fuck you all to death. I'm taking it. (*to* PAUL) You. Drop your gun.

> PAUL *obeys.*

**STEVIE:**  Okay. Now everyone else drop their guns.

> *They look at each other.*

**GINA MAE:**  It's possible no one else has a gun, Stevie.

**STEVIE:**  Shit. Was I born yesterday. Am I in charge or ain't I. Now everyone drop their guns or someone dies.

> GINA MAE, MARY, *and* JANE *take out pistols. Drop them.*

**STEVIE:**  Holy shit. I was right. Okay I'm on a roll. I'm gonna win. I'm really gonna win. Awk. Awk. Ah shit … Now stop that you crazy bitch. Awk!

*Slowly the arm holding* STEVIE*'s gun is moving, bending until the gun is at his temple.*

**STEVIE:** Stop it! Stop it! Jesus awk.

*Suddenly* STEVIE *begins to sob. The sobbing becomes a whimper as* STEVIE *slowly crumples onto the ground where he remains whimpering almost inaudibly. Everyone looks at* GINA MAE.

**GINA MAE:** I'd like to take responsibility for that. But I think he did it to himself. The man has such low self esteem his sub-conscious just couldn't handle the idea of him winning at anything and took the necessary steps to prevent it. I mean if anybody was wondering.

**TONY:** I was wondering.

**PAUL:** Me too.

MARY *is leaning over.* PAUL *picks up his gun quickly.*

**PAUL:** Leave that gun where it is, Mrs. Raft.

**GINA MAE:** Good for you Paul. Now where were we.

**JANE:** Fixing the wounded life force, Mom. You were about to explain to her how she's going to do it.

**GINA MAE:** Yes. Well money of course is the answer as it so often is. Lots of it. From you, Mrs. Raft. Five million a month let's say for an indefinite period.

**MARY:** You're in over your head. That's an incredible amount of money you're talking about. You're in the process of pushing me into a position which will allow me no alternative but to lash out at you.

**GINA MAE:** We'll chance it. After all we have your son. And we're keeping him.

**MARY:** For how long.

**GINA MAE:** I want a community centre. I want two new parks. I want low cost housing. I want a shelter for the homeless and the mistreated. I want big bright wonderful stores where people can get useful products at reasonable prices. I want halfway houses for people who are trying to re-enter the world from the unfortunate darkness of their circumstances. I want a throbbing, connecting, living, creative neighbourhood. I want a nice little place for my daughter to live. And I'm afraid you're going to have to pay for it ... No

one else will. I mean if you can convince some of your lofty
official friends to chip in, good for you. As for how long, well
as long as it takes. In the meantime Tony stays with us. We're
going to put him somewhere comfortable where you can't
find him.

**MARY:**   He's the only son I have left. I won't leave him with you.

**TONY:**   It's okay, Mom, I don't really mind.

**MARY:**   Please be quiet.

**TONY:**   But, Mom—

**MARY:**   I'm begging you to be quiet, Tony. I'm begging you not
to make me angry with you.

**TONY:**   But Mom she talks to me. She puts interesting things in
my brain. (*to* GINA MAE) Maybe you'll let me help plan things.
I've got a knack. You've obviously got a dream Gina Mae. I'm
sensitive to dreams. (*to* MARY) I'll make good use of the time,
Mom. I promise.

**MARY:**   But Tony. There are other people we have to keep happy.
We have a huge family if you remember. They won't wish me
to give these people so much money just to get you back.
Some of our family members aren't very fond of you, Tony.
Some of them think you're a flake. I'm being pushed into a
very awkward position here. It won't work. It's a plan
conceived by a madwoman. Okay!! Okay, to hell with it!
Everyone reach for their goddamn guns and let's just shoot
it out!!

> *They all panic.* GINA MAE *and* MARY *wind up struggling for the same
> gun.* DIAN *comes out of the darkness holding her I.D. over her head.*

**DIAN:**   Everyone stay very calm here. You're looking at the police
here. I'm here in an official capacity so everyone stay very
calm.

> DIAN *separates* MARY *and* GINA MAE. *Takes the gun.*

**DIAN:**   Now what seems to be the problem.

**GINA MAE:**   She doesn't like my plan.

**DIAN:**   Well I like it. It has scope. Courage. And it seems deeply
connected to a kind of popular fantasy.

> DIAN *whistles.*

**DIAN:**   Okay boys.

MICHAEL *and* ROLLY *appear out of the darkness.*

**DIAN:** Both these guys wound up at headquarters wanting for some reason to make confessions. They confessed for hours. But we decided it was best if we didn't understand what they were talking about. Next we decided to find out where they belonged and get them out of our hair. Now who belongs to who here. Hurry up. If they don't get claimed, they get put away.

**PAUL:** That one's my brother.

**DIAN:** Great. (*to* MICHAEL) You over there.

MICHAEL *goes over next to* PAUL.

**DIAN:** How about this one … No takers? (*to* ROLLY) I'm sorry. You're police property. Get used to it. I mean we can't just let you wander the streets unattended.

**JANE:** Mom?

**GINA MAE:** He's an awesome responsibility.

**JANE:** You said you'd try.

**GINA MAE:** I don't think I can do it alone.

**JANE:** I'll help.

**GINA MAE:** Really? You're such a thoughtful person, Jane. I'm so proud of you. Okay. I'll take him.

**DIAN:** Great. Over there, Rolly.

ROLLY *goes over to* GINA MAE.

**ROLLY:** Thanks, Gina Mae.

**GINA MAE:** You'll have to work. We're homeless you know. Your friends destroyed our life and we've got a lot of lost ground to make up.

**ROLLY:** They're not my friends. I'm just a victim. This lady cop explained it all to me on the way over. Turns out it goes way back in history. I'm a victim of those goddamn revolutions. You know, the industrial revolution and the technical revolution too. Hey, what's wrong with Stevie. Why's he look so sad.

**GINA MAE:** Ask *her.* (*points to* DIAN) She's the expert. Maybe he's a victim of the technical revolution too.

**DIAN:** Excuse me. I'm not finished yet. The man on the garbage
looks out of place. Untie him.

**PAUL:** (*to* GINA MAE) Should I.

**DIAN:** I know who you are, Mr. Gallagher. I'd think a man with
your background would have more respect for police
authority. Now untie him.

**TONY:** I don't want to be untied.

**DIAN:** Sure you do. (*to* PAUL) Do it. (*smiles*) Make my day.

> PAUL *proceeds to untie* TONY. TONY *resists but finally* PAUL *succeeds.*
> DIAN *turns to* MARY.

**DIAN:** Well this is a really fine  mess you've gotten us all into. I
thought you were warned.

**MARY:** I was taking appropriate measures.

**DIAN:** You were being shafted, lady. (*to* TONY) You. Over there
with your mother.

> TONY *goes over to* MARY.

> *Pause.*

> DIAN *walks slowly around. Stopping briefly at each group. Winds up in
> the middle. Takes out some gum.*

**DIAN:** So what we have here basically is conflict between
families. I mean if you simplify it. Let's do that. Let's simplify
it, so we can all find a way out. Now like I said before I like
that lady's plan.

**GINA MAE:** Thank you.

**DIAN:** It's not perfect though. It needs clarification. The money
is the problem. If the money just goes haphazardly from that
family to that family and then to that family (*points to* PAUL
*and* MICHAEL) to design and build all those wonderful
facilities well, you can imagine the questions. The public
revelations. Any solutions?

**TONY:** Tunnels!

> *They all look at him.*

**DIAN:** I've got one. A foundation. A legal beautiful
philanthropic foundation. The Raft Foundation. (*to* MARY)
Do you like the sound of that. The money will pass from the

Raft family to the Raft Foundation to the Sabatini family to the Sabatini Rebuilding Fund. It's a beautiful solution. Trust me.

**MARY:** It was my intention to one day start such a thing.

**PAUL:** Sure it was.

**MARY:** There are tax benefits to be had. I won't debate your inference beyond admitting that. The point is any such. foundation will be initiated in good time of my own free will. I will not do it under duress.

**DIAN:** You will do it under amazing and relentless duress. You will do it. Or you will be dispossessed of all your holdings in this city. I speak with authority here. It was given to me. I'm using it. Understand?

*Pause.* DIAN *goes to* MARY. *Hands her a piece of paper.*

There's a telephone number on that paper you could call to confirm my authority. I know you recognize that telephone number ... Do you understand now?

**MARY:** Yes.

**DIAN:** (*to* GINA MAE) Do you understand.

**GINA MAE:** You're hard to read. What are your true motives here. You're incredibly difficult to read.

**DIAN:** I'm just following orders. Doing my duty. Cleaning up the mess. Do you want the money from this lady's foundation or not? Yes or no. Fast now. This is a onetime offer.

**GINA MAE:** Yes.

**DIAN:** Good. An agreement. There are conditions, of course. This is the most important one—silence. Everyone understand silence?

*They all nod.*

**DIAN:** You know, I think we can make an exception of this five million, Mrs. Sabatini. Take it. Get started on something. A park would be nice. I've always liked parks.

GINA MAE *nods.* JANE *gets the suitcases.* DIAN *is collecting all the guns.*

**DIAN:** Life in the big city, eh. Some people love it. Some people just live it ... (*pinches* ROLLY's *cheek*) Keep in touch. (*starts off*) See ya.

*She is gone.*

*Long pause.*

MARY *is staring at* GINA MAE.

**GINA MAE:** Wow that's some look you're giving me, lady. How'd you get so filled up with negativity. You have such nice clothes. Apparently you have a big family. Where's the destructive impulse come from. And the cruelty. Usually it's stupid people who are as cruel as you. Have you considered changing your diet. Making new friends.

**MARY:** Come on, Tony. We're leaving.

**TONY:** Go ahead. I'll catch up.

MARY *starts off. Stops. Looks over her shoulder at* GINA MAE.

**MARY:** You and I will meet again.

**GINA MAE:** I hope so. Maybe sometime when I haven't had my house blown-up around me. When my senses are sharper. I'd love to know what makes you tick.

MARY *leaves.*

**PAUL:** Go with your mother, Tony. We don't want you here.

**TONY:** That's just a passing phase. (*to* GINA MAE) Promise you'll get in touch when you start to work. Anything that has to do with the future of this city I want in on. I've got the know how. I can be useful. Call me. Or better still just pop into my brain sometime. You're invited. That's an open invitation.

*He leaves.*

**GINA MAE:** Jane. Take ten thousand dollars of that money and put it in Stevie's pocket.

**JANE:** Why?

**GINA MAE:** I want Rolly to take Stevie to the airport and send him as far away as possible. The money will help him stay away. Is that all right with you Rolly?

JANE *sets about obeying her mother.*

**ROLLY:** If that's the situation, that's the situation Gina Mae. You sure you don't want me to go with him. I won't even take any money. I'd just disappear if that's what you want.

**GINA MAE:** It's up to you.

**ROLLY:** It is? Really? Okay, I'll stay. I really want to be a good person.

**GINA MAE:** Rolly, please. It's been a long day.

**ROLLY:** Okay I don't give a shit about being a good person. I just don't have the legs for a life of crime anymore. I'll be staying cause it's my only choice.

**GINA MAE:** That's a good enough reason, Rolly. This isn't church. We're not asking purity of thought from you here. We're just asking you to stop being destructive.

*ROLLY has STEVIE on his feet now, and is shaking him. Slaps him.*

**STEVIE:** Hey, hey. What's goin' on here.

**ROLLY:** You're leaving, boy. You're going far away.

**STEVIE:** Says who.

**ROLLY:** You got no choice.

**STEVIE:** Says who. Are you coming.

*ROLLY is pulling STEVIE off.*

**ROLLY:** No. I get to stay.

**STEVIE:** How come. Hey how come you get a choice to stay. Get fair. Come on. Why am I the only guy who never gets a fuckin' choice. Come on. Says who.

*They are gone. PAUL goes to GINA MAE. Hugs her. She looks at him oddly. He breaks away. Puts his hands in his pockets. Goes over to the garbage. Stares at it.*

**MICHAEL:** Paul?

**PAUL:** Shut up.

**MICHAEL:** It's just that I'd like to take this opportunity to apologize to you all and offer an explanation.

*GINA MAE turns on him.*

**GINA MAE:** Stupid man! Go back to your expensive car and your expensive house. You should have known better. Everything you have in your life should have made you a better person!

**MICHAEL:** I don't have an expensive car. My wife and kids have expensive cars. They also have an expensive four-wheel-drive all-terrain vehicle which they share … I drive a Plymouth Horizon. It's not a bad car. I'm not complaining, I'm just—

**GINA MAE:** Go home. Think about what you've done. Mr. Raft told us all about you. You let yourself be bought. Go home. Stay indoors for awhile. Be miserable!

MICHAEL *looks at* PAUL. PAUL *looks away.* MICHAEL *shrugs. Leaves.*

**JANE:** That was kind of harsh, Mom. Relatively speaking, I mean.

**GINA MAE:** He needed it. Basically he's a good boy. I was just spanking him a little.

**PAUL:** Who was that guy. He's not my brother. He's not even human ... How'd he get to be like that. How could he have been in with those people. I have to ... I've got to ... (*sits on the garbage bags*) ... think.

**GINA MAE:** Pick up the suitcases, Jane. We're going to your sister's.

**JANE:** Which one.

**GINA MAE:** You choose. They're all the same to me.

*They start off.*

**PAUL:** What about me.

**GINA MAE:** You'll live.

**PAUL:** That's it? After all we've been through together ...

GINA MAE *stops.*

**GINA MAE:** What do you want from me. You look great. You haven't had any nose bleeds. You're not having stomach pains ... Listen. Go home. Continue your illustrious career. Get on with your life. You're the least of my problems.

GINA MAE *starts off.*

**PAUL:** I didn't know you only thought of me as a problem.

**GINA MAE:** Relax. You'll be fine. If there's a good reason for it we might meet again sometime.

GINA MAE *catches up with* JANE. *Takes one of the suitcases. They start off.* PAUL *stands.*

**PAUL:** Yeah but ...

**GINA MAE:** Professionally, I mean. I might need you to do some work for us.

PAUL: Yeah but ... Well I feel there's something that isn't ... being completed here. I thought we meant something to each other. I thought we made a connection. You know, a spiritual bond.

GINA MAE: (*leaving*) There you go again. Like I said. This isn't a church. It's just the ongoing rhythm of existence. it sometimes skips a beat or two.

*They are gone.*

PAUL: She's gone. She just ... left. (*sits*) Come on. She didn't even say— (*feels his stomach*) Ooh, what's that. A pain. No ... not really a pain. A twinge. (*stands, shouts off*) Hey wait! I've got a twinge! ... (*shakes his head*) Pathetic. "Hey wait I've got a twinge." Pathetic. (*sits, looks around*) Hey wait, I've got a twinge. (*chuckles, smells something ... stands, smells himself*) Man, I need a bath ... Hey ... (*shouts off*) Hey wait, I smell! ... Hey wait I ... I'm losing my hair. I'm putting on weight. I'm—I'm not as smart as I thought I was. I'm ... I'm ... I'm a bad dancer. (*chuckles, sits again*) I liked that one. Bad dancer. That'll get her back ... (*laughs*)

*Blackout.*

*End.*

# Love and Anger

*Love and Anger* was first produced in Toronto by The Factory
Theatre. It opened on October 11, 1989 with the following cast:

PETER 'PETIE' MAXWELL   Peter Blais
GAIL JONES   Dawn Roach
ELEANOR DOWNEY   Clare Coulter
JOHN 'BABE' CONNER   Benedict Campbell
SEAN HARRIS   Hardee T. Lineham
SARAH DOWNEY   Nancy Beatty

Director: George F. Walker
Production Designer: Peter Blais
Lighting Designer: Peter Freund
Original Score: Lesley Barber

*Persons*
**PETER 'PETIE' MAXWELL**, fifty
**GAIL JONES**, early twenties
**ELEANOR DOWNEY**, mid-forties
**JOHN 'BABE' CONNER**, late forties
**SEAN HARRIS**, early fifties
**SARAH DOWNEY**, late thirties

*Place*

A damp grimy office in the basement of an old building on the fringe of the downtown area. Contains a desk, several chairs, a small couch, a few filing cabinets. There are a few small windows looking onto the street above. There are several metal bookcases half-filled with books. There are more books in several cartons on the floor. There is a tiny outer office stage left. The door to this office usually remains open, but we should see only a small portion of it. And there is a conveyor belt which runs up the wall, under the windows, to a trap door leading to the street.

*Note*

An intermission could be placed between Scenes Four and Five.

# Love and Anger

PETER 'PETIE' MAXWELL, *a fifty-year-old in an often worn, slightly rumpled, quality suit. Loose tie. Glasses. Sitting behind his desk. Fiddling with a cigarette.* GAIL JONES, *twenty-two, in jeans and a baseball jacket, sits in a chair in front of the desk.*

**MAXWELL:** The law is vulgar. Just like religion. Vulgar things both of them. Institutions corrupted by their own self importance. I'm immune to their seductive power. I've been around too long. Seen a lot of so-called illegal activity. Seen too much of it to believe it's just deviant behaviour. Anyway, more times than not, these days I come down in favour of the deviants. I'm not talking about the violent now. Especially not about the sexually violent. Violent sexual deviants I've got no time for. I don't want them executed or anything, but I think we have to construct a system of mutual protection. Us from them. And them from themselves. I'm in favour of increased government spending in the area of prison reform, medical facilities for the criminally dysfunctional. That sort of thing. You follow me so far?

**GAIL:** No.

**MAXWELL:** I'm talking about your situation vis-à-vis my situation.

**GAIL:** Nothing you've said in the last half hour has anything to do with my situation. I just want my husband out of prison.

MAXWELL *stands. Leans against the desk.*

**MAXWELL:** I was talking about the law. Trying to let you know that even though I'm constrained by it, I'm not impressed by it. The law is vulgar in its rigidity. Insensitive to the nuance of human existence. Derived and constructed from knowledge within a narrow historical corridor. In short, it's in love with itself. You'll get no true satisfaction from the law. You're marginal. Your cause is marginal. Outside the corridor, so to speak.

GAIL:  He's innocent.

> MAXWELL *picks up a cane which is lying on his desk. And starts to move around. He has a slight limp. During the course of the play he sometimes uses his cane, sometimes he doesn't.*

MAXWELL:  More and more I hear that word less and less. I spend a lot of time in courtrooms and I can tell you that that word has definitely fallen out of fashion. It even makes some judges cringe. I advise you not to use the word 'innocent' in front of anyone with real power.

GAIL:  He didn't break into those places the way they say he did … I mean he did. But he didn't want to. He was forced.

MAXWELL:  I know. I've read the transcript. I was impressed by your testimony. I believe you when obviously no one else does. That's why I called you back. I just want to make the situation clear.

GAIL:  You're not. It's not clear. You're failing at making it clear.

MAXWELL:  It's complex. I'm expressing the complexity before I attempt the clarification. Any fool could rob the situation of complexity and then clarify an essentially fraudulent simplicity.

GAIL:  Okay. Do that. I don't mind. I won't hold it against you.

MAXWELL:  Well there's our problem. We have two situations here. Yours of course is the one most urgent. But mine is the more persistent. You want your husband out of prison. I want to undermine the entire institutional bias of our culture. Now I believe it's possible we have a serendipitous union of intention here but you'll have to allow me to proceed in my own way.

GAIL:  And what will that be. Your way?

MAXWELL:  Trickery. I'm going to deke the legal establishment right out of its pants. For example. You say he was forced to make those break-ins by a couple of seedy hoods. Now normally I'd have to prove that. But quite simply that's impossible. We'd have to get the hoods to testify against themselves. No doubt they're stupid men but even that kind of hopeless maudlin stupidity has limits. No, I favour a solution that would involve blackmailing a judge with some invented indiscretion. Getting him to grant an appeal to save his own reputation. Perhaps even getting him to recommend a financial compensation for wrongful imprisonment. More and more I've come to believe you have to take money away from these people and their system in order to be truly satisfied. I mean it's the thing they and their system value most.

GAIL: I've got to ask you a question now. Don't take it the wrong way. Are you a ... crooked lawyer.

MAXWELL: In the strictest meaning of that term, yes. But remember the strictest meaning is the meaning of the strict—i.e. the law. The better truth is that I'm one of the few revolutionaries in Western civilization. A hidden force. You have, in a sense, hitched your wagon to a political imperative. We are about to become history in the making. How do you feel about that.

GAIL: Not too good, really ... Sounds like trouble. I don't want trouble. I just want my husband out of jail.

MAXWELL: Don't you want a shiny new future ... for you and your husband.

GAIL: Yes. I do.

MAXWELL: And what about the rest of the marginals. The millions of others in your situation. Or in situations even worse.

GAIL: What about them.

MAXWELL: If you could, would you help them.

GAIL: I guess.

MAXWELL: You're a good soul. I could tell from the heartbeat of your testimony. The love you have for your husband is just one arm of a many-armed beast. Full of compassion for everything in the world that needs love. Am I right.

GAIL: Are you right.

MAXWELL: I hope I'm right. Trust me. Do you trust me.

GAIL: No.

MAXWELL: Do you *want* to trust me.

GAIL: Yes.

MAXWELL: That's a start.

*A light is turned on in the outer office.*

Eleanor. Could you come in here for a moment, please. (*returns to the desk. Sits on the edge. Near* GAIL) Can you write.

GAIL: What do you mean.

MAXWELL: Can you read. Can you write.

GAIL: Sure. What kind of a question is that.

MAXWELL: Please don't be offended. I see lots of people who can't you know. Illiteracy is a problem.

GAIL: Yeah, well it's not my problem.

> ELEANOR DOWNEY *Comes in. She is middle-aged. A bit younger than* MAXWELL. *Conservatively dressed. Carrying a bag of cleaning supplies.*

ELEANOR: Can I help you with something, Mr. Maxwell.

MAXWELL: Eleanor. This is Gail Jones. Gail. This is Eleanor. Eleanor works with me. She's part of my team, my movement.

ELEANOR: I'm his secretary.

MAXWELL: That's her cover. She's actually the heart and soul of my operation.

ELEANOR: I'm just his secretary. (*to* MAXWELL) Please. I've asked you before. Don't involve me in whatever it is you're up to these days. I have problems of my own.

MAXWELL: (*to* GAIL) She doesn't trust you. When she trusts you she'll tell you the truth about herself.

ELEANOR: Please.

MAXWELL: Gail. I want you to go with Eleanor. She'll make a little space for you at her desk. She'll give you a pen and paper. She'll give you a coffee, although strictly speaking that's not part of her job, and she'll help you if you're having any difficulty completing your task.

GAIL: I have a task? Listen I don't—

MAXWELL: I want you to write about yourself. And your husband.

GAIL: About the break-ins?

> MAXWELL *reaches into his desk drawer. Takes out a chain of coloured paper clips. Begins to finger them.*

MAXWELL: Yes, Eventually. But don't start there. Start earlier. Write about your lives. Your needs. Your fears. Your beliefs …. Tell your story. Don't worry about style, structure, resolution. I can work on that later. Just think of it as a first draft. Something from deep inside the heart. Let it resonate. You know what I mean by resonate?

GAIL:  I know what resonate means!

MAXWELL:  So let it resonate.

> MAXWELL *is adding paper clips to the chain.*

GAIL:  (*to* ELEANOR) Is he really a lawyer.

ELEANOR:  Well he was once one of the most brilliant in the country. But he's had a … Yes. He's a lawyer.

> ELEANOR *goes to* MAXWELL. *Grabs the paper clips from him.*

GAIL:  (*to* MAXWELL) If I do this. This writing. Will it help you get Dave out of prison.

MAXWELL:  I'd rather not answer that question right now.

> GAIL *looks at* ELEANOR.

ELEANOR:  Don't worry, Gail. I'm sure Mr. Maxwell knows what he is doing. Go into my office, dear. I'll be with you in a minute.

> GAIL *leaves.* ELEANOR *turns. Sits opposite* MAXWELL.

Did you take your medication.

MAXWELL:  Yes. Yes I did. Don't worry. I actually do know what I'm doing. We are now officially embarked upon phase two. Do you want me to explain phase two for you.

ELEANOR:  What was phase one.

MAXWELL:  The obvious. I was a lawyer. I defended the obviously guilty. And the obviously not guilty. You typed. You answered the phone. You prepared affidavits. Where did it get us. Where did it get the world. What did we accomplish.

ELEANOR:  It was a job. We did our jobs.

MAXWELL:  It was death. Death was surrounding us like a demon inevitability. I suffered a stroke. It was something I could have done without, but I decided to turn it to my advantage. My brain is new. The stroke … and … (*takes another chain of paper clips from his pocket*) … a little therapy, gave me a new brain.

ELEANOR:  The stroke actually destroyed part of your brain.

MAXWELL: Well it was a part I didn't need anyway. My ability to communicate wasn't affected. My ability to communicate was somehow enhanced.

ELEANOR: That could be a matter of opinion. In any event, medically speaking, you're an invalid.

MAXWELL: Medicine is number four on my hit list. Right after law, religion, government.

ELEANOR: How did religion get on that list. Religion is a comfort to many people, myself included.

MAXWELL: I'm not talking about all religions. Just the religions of fear.

ELEANOR: Are we discussing phase two now.

MAXWELL: We're in the preamble ... And what about you. Your life is in pieces. Tiny pieces. Shattered glass. Here and there. Random. Nothing but a—

ELEANOR: Please.

MAXWELL: Your sister. I was speaking about your sister. We have to help Sarah. She's part of it. She'll be included. She's your problem. She's my problem. She's society's responsibility.

ELEANOR: She's schizophrenic. She can't be helped. She can only be monitored. They've convinced me.

MAXWELL: They?

ELEANOR: The doctors.

MAXWELL: Never let them convince you. Their confidence is spellbinding. But it's just there to hide their disappointment. Trust me. (*hugs her*) Please don't give up on her.

ELEANOR: I'd better go check on Gail.

MAXWELL: Gail ... She's a good soul. Her husband was framed, shafted, railroaded. She's an issue. She's a cause.

ELEANOR: She's a human being. And she's scared about what's happened to someone she loves. You scare her too. I don't think you should talk like that to her anymore. Talk like you used to talk to your clients.

MAXWELL: I patronized them. I pissed on their ingrained intelligence.

ELEANOR: Sometimes that's better.

*She leaves.* MAXWELL *hears something up in the street. Gets a chair.*
*Takes it over under the window. Stands on it. Taps on window.*

**MAXWELL:**  Hey. You. Get out of that garbage. There's nothing in
that garbage you want. Have a little self-respect. Come on!
Self-respect! Try it out!

*A commotion in the outer office.* JOHN 'BABE' CONNER *comes in.*
*In his late forties. Well dressed.*

**CONNER:**  Are you Peter Maxwell.

**MAXWELL:**  They used to call me Peter. They call me Petie now.

ELEANOR *comes in. Visibly upset.*

**ELEANOR:**  I want to call the police about this man. He laid
hands on me.

**MAXWELL:**  (*advancing on* CONNER) You should be shot! In
primitive societies they had exquisite rituals of pain designed
for people like you. (*to* ELEANOR) Didn't they.

**ELEANOR:**  I don't know.

**MAXWELL:**  (*to* CONNER) What's wrong. Some trouble with
mummy!? A little kindergarten Freudian encounter with a
distant but alluring teacher? We don't care!

**CONNER:**  She was in my way. She wouldn't move. I just helped
her back into her chair. Control yourself, man.

**MAXWELL:**  You're a bully. I hate you! She hates you too! Call the
police, Eleanor.

**ELEANOR:**  Good idea. (*leaves*)

**CONNER:**  You people are pretty sensitive. I don't want the police
involved. Don't you know who I am. Don't you recognize me.

**MAXWELL:**  Sure. You're John Conner. I read your newspaper
every day. It's painful. But I figure someone has to monitor
the crap you publish.

**CONNER:**  Yeah I know how you feel about my paper. The whole
city knows how you feel about my paper. That's why I'm here.

**MAXWELL:**  Not so fast. You owe my associate an apology. On
second thought we'll take money. One hundred dollars.

**CONNER:**  I'm not giving you any money. You're a clown. People
told me you were probably just some kind of deranged
clown. And they were right.

**MAXWELL:** Two hundred dollars. And fast. Eleanor's on the phone.

**CONNER:** No way.

**MAXWELL:** You physically assaulted my associate. A respectable woman with an unblemished record of public and private service ... It will make the front page. Not in your paper of course. The front page of your paper is reserved for inflammatory headlines and pictures of people tormented by agonizing personal grief. Three hundred dollars!

**CONNER:** What makes you think I can be ... (*looks toward the outer office*) Two hundred.

**MAXWELL:** Put it on the desk.

> CONNER *pulls a roll of bills from his pocket. Peels a couple of bills off the pile. Tosses them on Maxwell's desk. Sits in Maxwell's chair.* MAXWELL *puts the money in his jacket pocket. Picks up his phone. Pushes a button.*

Eleanor. You call the police yet? ... Well call them back. Tell them it might have been a mistake. I'll keep you posted ... You're in my chair by the way. How's Gail doing ... Well she's probably all tied up by syntax. The hell with syntax. Tell her that for me. (*hangs up*)

> MAXWELL *looks at* CONNER. CONNER *stands.*

So what can I do for you, Babe. That's what your friends call you, isn't it. Babe? Because you love baseball. Right?

**CONNER:** We have a problem. You and I have a problem. it's getting out of hand.

**MAXWELL:** How's that, Babe.

**CONNER:** Well in the first place—

**MAXWELL:** Want to sit down, Babe?

**CONNER:** In the first place, we know you're responsible for defacing our street boxes.

**MAXWELL:** That's a serious charge. (*takes a can of spray paint from a desk drawer. Slams it down on the desk*) You have proof?

**CONNER:** Of course I've got proof. What do you think I'm doing here!

MAXWELL: I don't know. Maybe you came here to beat up my secretary. Maybe your secretary's on vacation. Maybe she's in the hospital—

CONNER: God, man. What's wrong with you. You talk like a … you talk like a dope addict.

MAXWELL: How the hell would you know how a dope addict talks. You want to find out. Hang around. Twenty percent of the people who come through that door are dope addicts. Look I haven't got time for small talk. What's your problem.

CONNER: You. Your personal little war against my newspaper. I want it to stop.

MAXWELL: Close the paper down. It'll stop then.

CONNER: Who do you think you are. I'm a businessman. I'm a legitimate publisher. I have rights. My company has rights.

MAXWELL: Your paper is a fascist rag. It panders to everything weak and uncertain and uninformed in the human race. It has the rights given to it by a society which is essentially indifferent to the weak, uncertain and uninformed. I no longer recognize this society or its governing body. I am a citizen of the new era. I call this the age of getting even. Your newspaper is history. I'm just getting started … You want to take action against me, go ahead. A public battle in court is just what I want. You get me charged with vandalism, or whatever. I turn the trial into a holy war.

CONNER: I have options.

MAXWELL: Could you be more specific.

CONNER: I have options. I didn't get where I am by letting people push me around. I have … options. I'm talking about things you might find personally hazardous.

MAXWELL: Of course you are. You're a Nazi.

CONNER: Hey watch your mouth. Where do you get off, using a word like that to describe me. You know what that word means to people?

MAXWELL: Deep in my heart. At the root of my tenuous connection to the essence of life, I believe you are a Nazi. Your particular place in the historical corridor allows you to modify your behaviour for appearances, but you are still a

Nazi. If you were put in a position of power in any society desperate for a violent purging you'd buy yourself a uniform—and you'd be a Nazi!

**CONNER:** I told you to watch your mouth! I hate that word, I just hate it.

**MAXWELL:** You see a few months ago I had occasion to stare into the benign eye of God. And as God shrugged and gestured sadly for me to come rest in purgatory for eternity unless I got my priorities straight, I made myself some promises. And this is one of them. If it looks like a Nazi, call it a Nazi!!

**CONNER:** You're in big trouble. You may be insane. But that won't save you. Get ready for the battle of your life. (*grabs the can of spray paint. Leaves*)

**MAXWELL:** Good advice.

GAIL *comes in.*

**GAIL:** Are you too busy to talk.

**MAXWELL:** Never. How are you doing.

**GAIL:** The thing is … Well … I'm mad. Writing about Dave and me and those hoods … it's making me mad.

**MAXWELL:** That's good. Get madder.

**GAIL:** No. I didn't come here to get mad. I came here to get results.

**MAXWELL:** No. Really. Keep going. It sounds exciting. And it'll help us accomplish our mission.

**GAIL:** So you're thinking about it.

**MAXWELL:** What.

**GAIL:** Dave's case. You're planning a strategy or something.

**MAXWELL:** No time for that. Strategies require thinking. Thinking just removes you from the only necessary thing. Feeling it. You know, the anger, the burning, the deep honest anxiety. Look, would you feel better if I told you to go home and leave it to me. I could do that.

**GAIL:** Well I'm not sure—

**MAXWELL:** I could do that, but I wouldn't agree to it if I were you. I haven't got a clue how to get your husband out of prison. Legally, strategically—any other way.

GAIL: You don't? That's depressing. Somehow I thought ... Well I just had a feeling you'd get him out.

MAXWELL: Oh I'll get him out. The new way. It starts with a picture in my mind. Already in my mind I see him free. See you both. Together. Happy. Doing well. You're working for a construction company. He's a nurse.

GAIL: He's a sheet metal worker.

MAXWELL: That's good too.

GAIL: Well he's had trouble getting a permanent job ... I don't know ... He gets ... frustrated. Maybe too frustrated ...

MAXWELL: It's going to be fine. Forget about strategies. Just trust me. Trust yourself for wanting to trust me. Trust the picture in my mind. But most of all, trust the anger we both feel about the injustice you're suffering. Because the anger is the only thing we really need. Okay Gail?

GAIL: Okay, Mr. Maxwell.

MAXWELL: Call me Petie. They all call me Petie. And they smile too. Oh yes they do.

*He hugs her. She looks up at him a bit suspiciously.*

*Blackout.*

## SCENE TWO

*Later that evening.*

MAXWELL *is pacing. He seems agitated. Drinking occasionally from a styrofoam cup, which he occasionally refills from a bottle of scotch on the desk.* SEAN HARRIS *is sitting in the chair watching him. He appears slightly younger than* MAXWELL. *A nice suit. Clean cut. He also has a styrofoam cup. But he is nursing his drink.*

**MAXWELL:** It's all out in the open now. We can't pull that secret society crap anymore. We live in a world which requires and demands that so-called professionals be accountable for their actions.

**HARRIS:** Nothing's changed. People in general have no true understanding of how the law works. They can't be allowed to let their frustrations destroy the very thing which keeps this society functioning.

**MAXWELL:** This society isn't functioning. And the 'secret' law society is largely to blame.

**HARRIS:** That's nonsense. Lawyers don't rob convenience stores. Mug crippled pensioners. Sell crack to eight-year-olds.

**MAXWELL:** You've become accessories after the fact. The adversarial approach to your work has all but destroyed any confidence the public has in you. If relatively innocent people keep getting railroaded and you keep putting guilty slime back on the street just because it puts another mark in your win column soon there'll be no faith in the legal system at all. And then what you'll have and what you'll deserve is street justice. The sweet smell of revenge. Vigilantes.

**HARRIS:** What a load of naive garbage. I can't believe we're even talking about these things. We used to talk like this when we'd just started law school.

**MAXWELL:** When you had principles.

**HARRIS:** When we knew nothing about the world, And what's all this 'you' stuff. Aren't you a lawyer anymore.

**MAXWELL:** I don't know.

**HARRIS:** Well are you practising or not. Is this depressing little hole in the ground a law office or isn't it. It says it is on the door.

**MAXWELL:** Yeah. Well, I couldn't think of any other designation. I'm working on it.

**HARRIS:** Are you all right. Are you fully recovered. Should you be drinking so much.

**MAXWELL:** Yes to all those questions.

**HARRIS:** Where's Eleanor.

**MAXWELL:** I don't know. Out buying cleaning supplies probably. She's desperate to find something to remove the grime in this place.

**HARRIS:** Who's that girl out there at her desk. A client?

**MAXWELL:** A friend.

**HARRIS:** I miss you, Peter. The other partners miss you.

**MAXWELL:** I'm touched. Tell them I'm touched for me.

**HARRIS:** Of course they're perplexed. They don't understand why you left.

**MAXWELL:** They don't understand why people don't all wear suits the same colour. They don't understand why some young people still fall in love without asking each other what their job prospects are. They don't 'understand' anything except their work. And they don't see that their work is part of a systematic oppressive machine which conspires to deprive people of the options and the knowledge which are their fundamental rights.

**HARRIS:** Have you become a communist or something. (*laughs*)

**MAXWELL:** Yes.

**HARRIS:** A communist?

**MAXWELL:** Or something.

**HARRIS:** You're talking about your former partners like they're soulless monsters. Most of those men have been your friends for twenty years.

**MAXWELL:** That wasn't me. My body was invaded by some external force. It happened in my second year at law school. Late at night in the library. I removed pages from a reference book with my Exacto knife. And do you know why.

**HARRIS:** Sure. So no one else could get access to them. So you'd do better. Place higher. We all did it, Peter.

**MAXWELL:** Up to that point in my life I had never done anything remotely like that. My parents brought me up to prize honour. Honour was a big thing to them. The force made me do it. The force was everything in our world. Ambition, competition, self-promotion. Powerful, seductive things made by their power and seductiveness into a living external entity. *It* entered me. *It* removed the pages from that book. *It* helped me graduate head of my class. Start that damn firm. Hire all those damn clones. Pretend to be their friend. It's dead now. I'm back! I'm reborn. I'm like a little kid—still half formed. But I'm growing. Fast. Do you understand what I'm talking about.

**HARRIS:** Yes.

**MAXWELL:** You do? Really? Don't humour me now, Sean. Do you really get what I'm saying here.

**HARRIS:** Well … I think so. Yes. You're looking for some kind of renewal. Some kind of—what's that word … spiritual … spiritual renewal.

**MAXWELL:** Good for you. So will you come work with me here? Get reborn? Start all over again.

**HARRIS:** No. Of course not. I'm going to enter politics. Run federally. I'm announcing my candidacy tomorrow evening at the office. I'd appreciate it if you didn't come. There's a party afterward at the club. You're welcome to attend *that* if you're … in the mood.

**MAXWELL:** That's what you came here to tell me.

**HARRIS:** I came here because you asked for a meeting.

**MAXWELL:** But you're a conniving bastard. You never go anywhere without your own agenda.

**HARRIS:** I was about to remind you how long we've been friends. But of course that wasn't really you was it.

**MAXWELL:** The small part of me that wasn't the external force. The small part that was still human always had a soft spot for you.

**HARRIS:** Really.

**MAXWELL:** Yeah. I think it's because basically you were unmotivated. Your privileged background, your inherited wealth somehow shielded you from the vile needs of others.

**HARRIS:** You mean I had charm.

**MAXWELL:** Yes. You were charming, in a very basic way. Charm isn't necessarily a bad thing ... Have another drink.

**HARRIS:** No. I'm fine.

**MAXWELL:** So ... Politics ... Interesting. Why ... Boredom?

**HARRIS:** Probably. Yes.

**MAXWELL:** I suppose you think that's reason enough.

**HARRIS:** Basically, yes ... I mean once you've attained a certain amount, climbed to the top of the mountain so to speak, even if you've had assistance, you take the opportunity to look around. Find new challenges ... new mountains so to speak. I'm still young. Still have something to—what's the word ... contribute. But of course you don't agree.

**MAXWELL:** Hmmm. Let's just say that there are certain areas of life where charm ceases to be ... charming ... and becomes ... well, disgusting. One might even say immoral. There are problems in this country, Sean. In the world. We expect our politicians to solve them. Perhaps you think that's naive.

**HARRIS:** Yes I do. Not without some genuine albeit sentimental romantic justification. But naive nevertheless.

**MAXWELL:** You'll probably get elected.

**HARRIS:** The climate seems right. I'm told my timing is good.

**MAXWELL:** You have a platform?

**HARRIS:** I have an issue.

**MAXWELL:** What is it.

**HARRIS:** The deficit, of course.

**MAXWELL:** Of course ... Anything else?

**HARRIS:** If we bankrupt the country all the rest is more or less meaningless. Even with your new philosophy, whatever it is, surely you must still understand that the economy is everything.

**MAXWELL:** The economy as it stands. As you and your kind define it.

**HARRIS:** Is there some other way of defining it. Are you talking about redistribution or something.

MAXWELL:  Or something … So you don't want me at your side when you announce. People will be puzzled. We've been a team a long time.

HARRIS:  The word's out about you, Peter. Nothing tangible. Just rumour. Most of it tied to your stroke.

MAXWELL:  They think I'm demented.

HARRIS:  Your behaviour in the last couple of months has been more than a bit eccentric. People haven't been blessed with a personal audience like I have. They don't know that you are 'reborn.' They think that maybe you're still very ill. This conflict with Babe Conner—

MAXWELL:  Nazi!

HARRIS:  Excuse me?

MAXWELL:  He's a Nazi. He must die … In a manner of speaking I mean. He must be laid to rest. And his influence with him.

HARRIS:  That might be difficult.

MAXWELL:  His newspaper is a cancer on the body politic.

HARRIS:  It's tacky yes. Badly written. Sensationalist. Even regressive. But well … who do you think reads that paper. Our people don't even give it a glance … Your people read it.

MAXWELL:  My people? Your people? Let's keep the distinctions a bit more abstract for now Sean. We don't want a class war here, do we. I mean all I'm looking for is a little damage control. An easing up on the exploitation. Getting him to stop taking dead aim at the lowest common denominator.

HARRIS:  He's a client.

MAXWELL:  Conner? Since when.

HARRIS:  He engaged us this morning.

MAXWELL:  Tricky bastard … So he's suing me.

HARRIS:  That's an option. There are several ways that option could be handled. You've left yourself wide open here Peter.

MAXWELL:  Libel?

HARRIS:  That's an option. I'm considering the possibilities.

MAXWELL:  You personally? You haven't litigated in years. Look, why don't you let someone else in the firm handle it,

especially if you're going to run for public office. The heat
I'm planning to generate from this thing could seriously
damage you. This thing is bigger than that little rag of
Conner's. This is the first step in the reorganization of an
entire culture! This is the beginning of the end of the secret
societies!

HARRIS: Knock it off. It's a civil suit. And you're dead meat.
You've been harassing the guy. You've put it in writing in his
competitors' papers. You've talked about it on cheesy
talk-shows. You've scrawled it across his billboards and his
street boxes. You've written outrageous, bullheaded,
unsupportable, inflaming crap about this guy, and you've
signed your name. You're defenceless.

MAXWELL: I have no assets.

HARRIS: Bull.

MAXWELL: I gave everything away. The house, car, stocks,
everything.

HARRIS: Come on. You don't seriously expect me to believe that.

MAXWELL: On an impulse. Pure. And childlike … it's all gone.
I'm immune. I have nothing. Except my name. And I'm
changing my name.

HARRIS: Why. Are you going into hiding.

MAXWELL: Just the opposite. Anyway I'm not changing my last
name. I'm changing my first name. I want people to call me
Petie. Not Peter. Petie!

HARRIS: Why.

MAXWELL: Petie Maxwell. It sounds better. Younger. More
unfinished. Like me … The way I am now. Call me Petie!
Try it!

HARRIS: Are you drunk. Have you just slipped over the edge
here, or what. We were talking about a possible law suit.

MAXWELL: You were threatening me. I know the routine. I just
wanted to let you know it wouldn't work. Go tell Conner it
didn't work. If you're lucky he'll fire you. Trust me. You
don't want to be associated with him. He's going down. The
name calling, that's just the beginning. This man has done
many nasty, illegal things. And I've got the stuff that's
eventually going to prove it.

**HARRIS:** What do you mean by 'stuff.' You mean hard evidence?

**MAXWELL:** I'm talking about a certain kind of ... information.

**HARRIS:** What.

**MAXWELL:** Can't tell. Privileged. For now.

**HARRIS:** How'd you get it.

**MAXWELL:** Just sat here. People came through that door and gave it to me. I moved my operation down to this sad and nearly forgotten part of the city, opened for business, and all sorts of quasi-exotic creatures came through my door. Most of them pathetic. Many of them helpless. Some of them purely evil. But they all had stories. We're talking about the dregs here, Sean. And some of them are privy to a lot of very damaging information. And they came in here and talked. About themselves mostly. About things that pertained to their own severe dilemmas. Arrested for drugs, arrested for petty theft, armed robbery, soliciting—the whole miserable gamut. But some of the names, the places, in their histories were from another world. I just wrote them down. Had them write them down. Conner's name came up quite a bit. Some of it rumour. A story overheard. That kind of thing. But that kind of thing can be followed up. Checked out. No one ever did before, that's all. No one ever burned inside enough, needed to grow enough. But then there was me. Trust me. Get him to fire you. He's going down. And so are some others. It's all part of phase two. The amazing rebirth of Petie Maxwell and the new era to which he is dedicated ...

> *Pause.*

> HARRIS *stands. Calmly puts his drink down on the table.*

**HARRIS:** So I have your word that you won't be there for my announcement tomorrow.

**MAXWELL:** Yes.

**HARRIS:** Good. Well it's been great seeing you again.

> HARRIS *puts out a hand.* MAXWELL *looks at it oddly. Then takes it. They shake. Continue to hold hands.* HARRIS *looks at his watch.*

Well I better run. I'm taking Sandra and the kids out to a movie.

**MAXWELL:** Very generous of you.

**HARRIS:** Is that a joke. I didn't get it.

**MAXWELL:** You don't 'take' your wife out to a movie anymore. You go together. I read that in a magazine a while ago. The magazine said married people became happier that way.

**HARRIS:** Too bad you're not still married to her yourself. You could check that theory out personally.

**MAXWELL:** The man I used to be didn't deserve a good marriage. Even to a jerk like Sandra. How are my kids by the way.

**HARRIS:** They're not your kids. They're mine. Remember?

**MAXWELL:** See what I mean. You'd been screwing my wife since law school and it took me twenty years to find out. I must have been a very distracted man. Did I ever tell you how much it hurt me when I found out about you and Sandra.

**HARRIS:** No ... You're not going to tell me now are you.

**MAXWELL:** It killed me a bit. It darkened my life. Made me feel like one of God's lowest creatures. A maggot under a rock. Made me throw up a lot. I threw up for six months.

**HARRIS:** I'm ... you know ... sorry.

**MAXWELL:** Can I kiss you.

**HARRIS:** What ... I don't understand.

**MAXWELL:** I just want to kiss you.

**HARRIS:** On the mouth?

**MAXWELL:** No actually. I'd like you to drop your pants. I want to kiss your ass. No really, it's important to me. I feel it's a way of finally completing my humiliation. Can I do that.

**HARRIS:** No you can't.

**MAXWELL:** Will you kiss mine then. In some ways that would be better. If I drop my pants would you give me a long wet kiss on my ass.

**HARRIS:** You're in deep trouble Peter. You should seek professional help.

**MAXWELL:** Relax. It was just a passing thought.

**HARRIS:** Right. Well. I really do have to be leaving.

**MAXWELL:** Go ahead.

**HARRIS:** You'll have to let go of my hand first. You're squeezing it.

*Pause.*

MAXWELL, *still holding* HARRIS*' hand, gets very close to his face.*

**MAXWELL:** Don't even think about it! Don't consider it for even one minute. If you are stupid enough to take what I've told you to Conner so you can make some Brownie points, I want you to put this into the gains and losses equation. I know stuff about you too. All those years of doing business together, Sean. The little shortcuts you sometimes took.

**HARRIS:** And you too.

**MAXWELL:** Yes. But I'm repenting. And what's more important ... I'm immune. Remember?

**HARRIS:** No one's immune. That's self-delusion. There are still things in this world you care about. People you care about. There's no way you got rid of everything. Now let go of my hand.

MAXWELL *obeys. Steps back.*

Thank you.

**MAXWELL:** Goodbye, Sean.

**HARRIS:** Goodbye ... Petie.

HARRIS *leaves.* MAXWELL *grabs a book. Throws it at the door.*

*Pause.*

**MAXWELL:** He's dangerous. I can't believe how dangerous he's become. He'll go to Conner. They'll form a pact. An ungodly alliance ... Is this the focal point ... Is this going to be a holy war. Is it?

MAXWELL *walks over to the window. Looks out.*

*Blackout.*

## SCENE THREE

ELEANOR, GAIL, *and* SARAH DOWNEY.

SARAH *is Eleanor's sister. A woman in a loose housecoat. Gym shoes. A knapsack on her back. Sitting cross-legged on the desk. Talking while the other two listen.* GAIL *is enthralled.* ELEANOR *is nervous, impatient.*

**SARAH:** Big tractor trailers. Hundreds of them. All painted white. Everything white. White tires. Hundreds of big white tractor trailers thundering down the highways. Looking for adventure. Looking for a place to take over. Surround. A small town, surrounded by tractor trailers is every small town's worst nightmare. And these guys know it. The guys who drive these things. Big beefy white guys who bought these tractor trailers and painted them white. Sold their houses to buy them, sold their Harley-Davidsons and their kids' roller skates, made their wives become prostitutes and cashed their baby bonus cheques, so they could buy their tractor trailers and form a club. A club that was big and fast and white and thunders down any highway to any destination and takes over. (*jumps off desk*) Big beefy mean white guys who hate little people. And little cars. But mostly they hate black people, and brown people and yellow people. So they surround a town and they take it over and they become the power. They're indestructible. They're armour-plated. They're full of hate. And now they've got a headquarters. A centre of operations. First thing they do is kill everyone who isn't beefy or white. Kill all the skinny people. And the two black people in town. And the old guy who owns the Chinese restaurant. Kill them openly. Kill them without fear. Because they're in control. They're free to be themselves. Free to be the one thing that's been hidden all these years. The big beefy mean white guys full of hate. Because some of them, most of them, aren't really big, don't look big, only have the big guy *inside* them. The big beefy guy inside them has been talking to them for years. Telling them to let him out. To do his thing. His necessary thing. First get me a machine he says. A big thundering machine, an operations base, a mobile base, a tractor trailer. Get it rollin'. Get some respect. Join up with others. Declare ourselves. Then get a permanent

home ... So they did. They got a town. They got it
surrounded. And word gets out. Soon it starts to spread.
Thousands of white tractor trailers banding together. Taking
over towns. Killing little people, brown people, everyone who
isn't beefy and white. It's a movement. It's happening
everywhere. It's out in the open. It's an accepted thing. It's
the way it is. We're surrounded. It's our turn to die ...

>    *Pause.*

**GAIL:**   Because we're not big and beefy? (*she laughs*)

**SARAH:**   Because we're not white. Because we're black.

>    GAIL *looks at* ELEANOR.

**ELEANOR:**   Gail is black, Sarah.

**SARAH:**   Yeah. That's right. I know she's black. That's why I'm
sharing this secret information. This information is for the
ears of our people only.

**GAIL:**   (*to* ELEANOR) I don't get it.

**ELEANOR:**   Sarah and I are black too, Gail. Perhaps you haven't
noticed. I mean Sarah *is ... black*. And I am Sarah's sister so—

**SARAH:**   So she's black too. It only makes sense. I can't be black if
she isn't black. Right, Eleanor.

**ELEANOR:**   Right. (*to* GAIL) And Sarah ... is ... *black*. Do you
understand, Gail.

**GAIL:**   Ah ... I guess.

**SARAH:**   Well look at me. Whatya mean 'I guess.' Look at me.
Isn't it obvious.

**ELEANOR:**   Yes.

**SARAH:**   I'm asking her!

>    *The phone rings in the outer office.*

**ELEANOR:**   That's our phone. Would you get it for me, Sarah.
Take a message.

**SARAH:**   I don't take messages. I only send messages. I can't be a
receptacle. It's dangerous to my health.

**ELEANOR:**   I don't want to talk to anyone. Mr. Maxwell has been
getting some very strange calls from some of his new breed
of clients. Just tell whoever it is we're not available.

**SARAH:** Strange calls? Threatening calls I bet. People threatening Petie. Okay, that I can handle.

SARAH *rushes out.*

**ELEANOR:** It's risky letting her answer the phone. But I had to talk to you alone.

**GAIL:** She thinks she's black?

**ELEANOR:** Well maybe she wants us to think she's black. Or maybe she just wants us to think she thinks she's black. It's hard to say … Or yes maybe in her mind, truly she's black.

**GAIL:** She's ill?

**ELEANOR:** Yes. But she's courageous. She's always been very courageous. The doctors think she has to have a way, even in her state, to manifest her courage. That her courage is still the most important thing to her.

**GAIL:** So she thinks it takes courage to be black.

**ELEANOR:** Well doesn't it dear.

**GAIL:** I don't know … It's not like we have a choice. I mean does it take courage to be what you are when there's no way you could be anything else.

**ELEANOR:** That's beyond me. Sarah is beyond me too. Even when she was well. Actually, looking back I'm not sure she was ever well. But she was always beyond me.

SARAH *comes on.*

**SARAH:** I'm back. Stop talking about me.

**GAIL:** We … weren't.

**SARAH:** Sure you were. I don't mind. Just don't do it to my face! I took a message. I made an exception just this once. It was someone looking for Petie. Sean Harris. Sounded smooth. Too smooth. Talking to him almost gave me the runs.

SARAH *hears* MAXWELL *coming. Hides behind the couch.* MAXWELL *comes in. Carrying two large pizza boxes.*

**MAXWELL:** It's a party. I've got the food. Double cheese. Double mushrooms. Double everything.

GAIL *gets up.*

**GAIL:** Did you see Dave.

MAXWELL:  I saw him. He saw me. We recognized each other
immediately. We talked. He told me his story. I told him
mine. His was truly painful. But mine was much longer ...
Well, more complex. Somewhere between his pain and my
complexity we reached a common ground.

   SARAH *stands.*

SARAH:  The commonality of complex pain. That makes sense.
It's the thing that ties us all together. All living things.
Regardless of race or religion.

MAXWELL:  Honey. You're out.

SARAH:  I escaped.

MAXWELL:  (*to* ELEANOR) Is that true.

ELEANOR:  She was released.

SARAH:  I had myself re-diagnosed. Obsessive-compulsive. I told
them I just wanted to wash my hands all the time. What harm
can that do.

   SARAH *and* MAXWELL *are approaching each other slowly.*

MAXWELL:  They bought that?

SARAH:  They're in a buying mood. Space is at a premium in that
place. Anyway I think of it as an heroic escape.

MAXWELL:  Well you're out. That's the only important fact. Saves
me the trouble of breaking you out. I was this close to doing
it too. Do you believe me.

SARAH:  I believe everyone.

   *They hug.*

ELEANOR:  (*to* MAXWELL) Tell Gail about her husband, for God's
sake. Can't you see her sitting there. Can't you see how
anxious she is. For God's sake, Peter.

GAIL:  Please!

MAXWELL:  He's fine. Says he's fine. He misses you.

GAIL:  I know he misses me. I know he says he's fine. I know all
that. I didn't come to you so you could tell me things I know.
How are you going to get him out of that place!

MAXWELL:  An appeal. A new trial.

ELEANOR:  Based on what.

**MAXWELL:** New evidence.

**GAIL:** What new evidence.

**MAXWELL:** Things which will soon come to light.

**ELEANOR:** What things.

**MAXWELL:** Things which I fabricate.

**ELEANOR:** Oh no. Come on now.

**MAXWELL:** Brilliant fabrications. Totally supportable. Riddled with detail. An impenetrable tapestry of cast-iron bullshit.

**ELEANOR:** You'll go to prison. You'll really help him that way. You'll find a common ground all right. You'll be playing checkers together for ten years.

**SARAH:** You won't like prison, Petie. Prison will be death for your neo-persona. Besides everyone spits in prison. They spit everywhere. Spit stains on the walls, the floors, on all the gym equipment—

**GAIL:** I'm getting another lawyer. I knew in my bones this was a mistake. All you've done for me is make me nervous. Make me nervous and make me write things. I've been sitting here for hours writing and trembling. I've got about a hundred pages of really shitty handwriting and all you've—

**MAXWELL:** A hundred pages?! I'm ecstatic. Where is it. Get it.

**GAIL:** No. I'm leaving.

**MAXWELL:** You can't leave. I'm your only hope. That is until Eleanor here realizes her potential.

**ELEANOR:** Leave me out of this.

**MAXWELL:** (*to* GAIL) I'm sorry. I wish there was someone better. But there isn't. There's just me. Fate's cruel like that sometimes. I wish I looked better. Bigger. I wish my voice was deeper. I wish I still had all my brain. But I don't. All I have is my growth potential. And my belief. I'll get Dave out of prison though. And I'll get him out the only way there is to get him out. By undermining the system that put him there.

**SARAH:** (*to* ELEANOR) Is Dave innocent.

**MAXWELL:** Don't answer that, Eleanor. We don't use the word 'innocent' around here any more. The simple fact is that he's far less guilty than the two sleazy hoods that the system let go.

**SARAH:** So you're just correcting an imbalance. I can relate to that. I love you.

**MAXWELL:** I love you too.

**SARAH:** (*to* ELEANOR) We love each other.

**ELEANOR:** I'm happy for you both.

**SARAH:** Don't get all sappy. Nothing's gonna come from it. He's only got about twenty minutes to live. And I'm incurably insane.

**ELEANOR:** We don't use the word insane, Sarah.

**SARAH:** I do. And I'm the expert.

**MAXWELL:** (*to* GAIL) Please stay. Please. Show me your writing.

**GAIL:** Why.

**MAXWELL:** I need it. I need the whole picture. I need to put your story together with Dave's story so that I can write the epilogue. Please get it. Please trust me.

**GAIL:** Oh, I hate this feeling. I feel like I've got no choice. Why.

**MAXWELL:** Because you're pathetic. Don't be offended. I'm the same way. We're all pathetic. Do you feel like you've got any real choice about anything Sarah.

**SARAH:** No.

**MAXWELL:** Do you Eleanor.

**ELEANOR:** Yes.

**MAXWELL:** Yeah, well Eleanor is less pathetic than the rest of us. Good for her. We might have to use Eleanor a little later. She might be the only one left standing. (*to* GAIL) I'll get the food out. You go get your writing. Okay?

**GAIL:** Yeah, I guess ... Okay.

GAIL *leaves.*

**MAXWELL:** Who wants pizza. I do. I do. You know I never ate pizza in my former life. It just wasn't done. Don't ask me why.

**ELEANOR:** Why would we want to ask you why. Is it important.

**MAXWELL:** It could be Eleanor. I don't know for sure.

**SARAH:** Yuk. Look at that stuff. All stuck together. I'm not eating that. If you want me to eat that you've got to separate everything.

**MAXWELL:** Sure. No problem.

**ELEANOR:** Give me her piece. I'll do it.

MAXWELL *hands* ELEANOR *a slice.*

**SARAH:** Take the mushrooms off the green peppers. Take the green peppers off the tomato slices. Move them over. Move them over!

**ELEANOR:** I'm trying!

**MAXWELL:** Any messages?

**ELEANOR:** Sean called.

**MAXWELL:** What's he want.

**ELEANOR:** Call him! Find out!

**MAXWELL:** You're a bit testy today, Eleanor.

**ELEANOR:** I wonder why!!

**SARAH:** It won't work! Look. It's just all sticking together. There's a mushroom deep inside that sauce. It's the cheese. It's ruining everything. Everything's sticking to the cheese! It's gotta go. Give it to me. I'm gonna wash it. Give it to me!

SARAH *grabs the slice.*

**ELEANOR:** There's a washroom down the hall.

**SARAH:** I know that! I've been here before, Eleanor.

**ELEANOR:** I was just—

**SARAH:** I'm not your child, Eleanor. Be careful you don't talk to me like your child. There is no gain in that attitude for either of us. (*starts off. Stops*) Anyone else want theirs washed.

**MAXWELL:** No. I'm fine.

**ELEANOR:** So am I.

**SARAH:** Well suit yourself. It's gonna form a big ball in your lower intestine. It'll sit there for weeks. But it's your life … it's your life!

*She leaves.* ELEANOR *bends over. Puts her head in her hands.*

**MAXWELL:** Cheer up. She seems much better.

**ELEANOR:** Be quiet. (*looks up*) What would you know about it.

**MAXWELL:** All those times I've visited her in the hospital these last few months. We've talked. We've looked into each other's souls. We have this uncanny communication. We don't always use words. Sometimes we just look at each other and nod ... slowly. Very slow nodding. Like this ... (*he demonstrates*) It's amazing.

ELEANOR: You're worse than she is.

MAXWELL: You think so? Well I don't feel so bad. So that should be good news to you. I mean in relative terms—

ELEANOR: Be quiet! Call Sean. Do some business. Act like a professional lawyer please. Just once or twice a day. Please. Call Sean!

MAXWELL: I'll get right on it.

> MAXWELL *picks up the phone. Dials.* GAIL *comes back in. Carrying three large legal-size yellow pads.*

GAIL: I think a lot of it's illegible. Especially the really personal parts. And there are tear stains. (*to* ELEANOR) Do you believe it. I cried like a baby a few times. It was awful.

MAXWELL: Sounds terrific, honey. I'll be right with you.

GAIL: (*to* ELEANOR) What's he doing.

ELEANOR: Calling his ex-partner.

GAIL: About Dave?

ELEANOR: I don't think so. (*to* MAXWELL) Is it about Dave, Peter.

MAXWELL: Dave who?

GAIL: Oh shit. (*sits*)

MAXWELL: Hello. Sean Harris please ... Yeah, it's Peter—Petie Maxwell. (*to* GAIL) I'll be right with you honey. Relax ... (*to* ELEANOR) Gee look at all those pages ... Looks great ... Hi Sean ... Yeah ... No ... No I haven't ... No ... That's right no. Yes ... Yes ... Yes! Oh. Good for you ... Good for him too ... Oh, really. What was that ... Say that again. Come on say it again. I just want to make sure I get it on tape. Yeah that's right ... I am. I'm taping you. Well ... What? ... The same to you I guess! (*he hangs up*) That man is turning into a psychopath. He threatened my life.

ELEANOR: He didn't.

MAXWELL: I've got it on tape.

ELEANOR: No you don't.

**MAXWELL:** Oh right. That was a bluff. I've got to be careful. I'm starting to believe in my own fantasies. Mostly I think that's a good thing, but there are times we have to be careful not to—

**ELEANOR:** Be quiet. What was it about. Conner?

**MAXWELL:** Yeah. The same things. But more desperate. 'Babe Conner's an important man. A powerful man. Untouchable.'

GAIL *starts flipping through her pad madly.*

**ELEANOR:** Well that's true. You know that. How can you fight him if you won't even acknowledge a simple truth about him.

**MAXWELL:** It's an implied truth. It's the implication that I'm fighting.

**ELEANOR:** Yes but—

**GAIL:** What was that name.

**ELEANOR:** What name, dear.

**GAIL:** The name he said just now. The powerful man's name.

**MAXWELL:** Conner.

**GAIL:** The first name.

**ELEANOR:** John.

**GAIL:** No he didn't say John. What was it.

**MAXWELL:** Babe. (*walking toward* GAIL)

**GAIL:** Yeah. Babe ... Some guy ... called Babe ... Some rich guy. Dave said those hoods were probably working for someone who—Here it is!

**MAXWELL:** Let me see that. (*grabs the pad from* GAIL. *Reads*)

**GAIL:** Who is he.

**ELEANOR:** (*stands*) Come on now. Let's be careful here.

**GAIL:** Who is he. Who is he!

MAXWELL *looks up.*

**MAXWELL:** He's dead meat! He's the end of an era. He's ... your husband's ticket out of prison.

GAIL *stands.*

**GAIL:** Really? You think so? How.

**MAXWELL:** These things in here. These things you wrote. Are they true.

**GAIL:** I don't know. What things. What I wrote about Dave and me ... our life together. That's true.

**MAXWELL:** These things the hoods said about the rich guy.

**GAIL:** They told Dave they've been doing crooked things for him for years. I don't know if that's true or not. Neither did Dave.

**MAXWELL:** Well why wouldn't it be true.

**ELEANOR:** I can't believe a man with your experience in criminal law is asking that question. Examine the source.

**MAXWELL:** You think crooks can't tell the truth? Crooks can lie. Crooks can tell the truth. Everyone get their coats.

**ELEANOR:** Why.

**MAXWELL:** We've got work to do. We've each got an assignment. We're spreading out. Get your coats.

GAIL *leaves.*

**ELEANOR:** What assignment. Spreading out where.

**MAXWELL:** It's a mission in search of the relative truth. I'll explain on the way out. (*throws Gail's pads on the desk*)

**ELEANOR:** I can't leave. What about Sarah.

**MAXWELL:** Sarah's fine. You're not her mother.

**ELEANOR:** Don't you start!

**MAXWELL:** You'll have to leave her alone sometime. You can't glue yourself to her. Do both of you a favour. Trust her. She is what she is. She'll do what she has to do.

**ELEANOR:** Easy for you. You're not responsible for her. I'm her legal guardian.

**MAXWELL:** So what! Big deal! Who gives a shit about that stuff anymore! It's linear. Legal guardian is a linear concept! Try being her sister. Come on. I need you.

MAXWELL *tries to push her out the door.*

**ELEANOR:** Let me just tell her we're leaving.

**MAXWELL:** No. She'll want to come with us. It's too dangerous.

**ELEANOR:** Wait a minute now! Who says danger is part of my job. I'm a legal secretary.

**MAXWELL:** No! How can you be a legal secretary! Not now. That's part of the linear past too. Think about it. We're just friends. Friends in the struggle. Okay, okay. You just go to the library for now. We'll include you in the dangerous part later.

**ELEANOR:** God help us all.

**MAXWELL:** Sure. If she has the time.

*They are gone.*

*Blackout.*

*Two hours later.*

*SARAH is sitting behind Maxwell's desk. Feet up. Reading Gail's story. Crying gently. Humming an African song. A knock on the outer door. Sound of it opening. Muffled voices.*

*HARRIS and CONNER come in. Overcoats, silk scarves. Look at SARAH. At each other.*

**HARRIS:** Excuse me? ... Excuse me?

**SARAH:** Be with you in a minute. Just want to finish reading this beautiful paragraph ... Beautiful and sad. This girl's a genius. Someone should tell her ... I'll do it. (*looks up*)

**HARRIS:** We're looking for Peter Maxwell.

**SARAH:** Not here.

**CONNER:** Yeah, we can see that. Is he coming back.

**SARAH:** Sure.

**CONNER:** When.

**SARAH:** Don't know.

**HARRIS:** Are you a friend of his.

*She looks at them for a moment.*

**SARAH:** Are you.

**CONNER:** (*to* HARRIS) Fuck him. Let's go.

**HARRIS:** I think it's worth one final effort all things considered. Don't you.

**CONNER:** Yeah. I guess.

**HARRIS:** (*to* SARAH) Do you mind if we wait.

**SARAH:** Sure. Wait. Sit on that couch.

**HARRIS:** Thanks. We know it's late. But we saw the lights on. I heard he works late. Sometimes even sleeps here.

*They take off their coats. They both have on black and white formal wear. SARAH bolts out of her chair.*

**SARAH:** Holy shit! You look like a couple of vampires! ... You can't walk around with those things on. Don't you realize the images those things conjure up.

**HARRIS:** We've just come from a function.

**SARAH:** You look like you've come from a dinner at the Reichstag. Some family affair of the Third Reich. You look like Goering. You look like Speer.

**CONNER:** (*to* HARRIS) What is all this Nazi crap around here. Are these people living in the goddamn past ... I mean, it's starting to really annoy me.

**SARAH:** Take them off. Take them off! ... Come on. They're scaring me. I'm gonna wet my pants or something. Jesus. At least loosen the ties. Undo a button or two. You look like machines. Nazi vampire machines. I'm getting scared. Look guys I really mean it ... Loosen your ties!!

HARRIS *does.*

**HARRIS:** (*to* CONNER *in a whisper*) Loosen your tie.

**CONNER:** What for.

**HARRIS:** She's scared. Look at her.

**CONNER:** That's her problem. It's a tie. It's just a tie.

**HARRIS:** So just loosen it. What's the big deal. It scares her.

**CONNER:** Why.

**HARRIS:** I don't know. Ask her.

**CONNER:** Ah. The hell with it. (*loosens his tie*)

**HARRIS:** (*to* SARAH) Better?

**SARAH:** A little ... So you were at a function. That's nice. I used to function ... Now I just dream. (*starts to read again*)

**CONNER:** What's she talking about.

**HARRIS:** I don't know.

**CONNER:** Who is she.

**HARRIS:** I don't know.

**CONNER:** Ask her.

**HARRIS:** You ask her.

**CONNER:** (*to* SARAH) Hey you! What are you doing here. Are you a client.

SARAH *looks up. Slowly.*

**SARAH:** Client? What made you ask that. Why didn't you ask if I was a lawyer. Does it look like I couldn't be a lawyer … for some reason.

**HARRIS:** Are you a lawyer.

**SARAH:** Yes.

**HARRIS:** You work with Mr. Maxwell?

**SARAH:** I'm his new partner. My name is Sarah Downey.

> *She stands, walks to them. Puts out her hand.* HARRIS *and* CONNER *look at each other. Shake with her in turn.*

**HARRIS:** Sean Harris.

**CONNER:** John … Conner.

**SARAH:** Perhaps I can help you. Are you looking for a lawyer.

**CONNER:** We're looking for Maxwell.

**SARAH:** You have … some reason you don't want to do business with me … You don't do business with black people?

**HARRIS:** I beg your pardon.

**SARAH:** Oh excuse me. I should have been more subtle. But sometimes the yoke slips you know. The beast escapes. Stands up straight. Tells it like it is,

> *She gives them a Nazi salute.*

**CONNER:** Let's get outta here.

**HARRIS:** Okay.

**SARAH:** Okay? … Okay okay. I've had my laugh. You guys are too much. Lighten up! I'm sorry for stringing you along. I don't know. Maybe it's the way you're dressed. It just brought out the mischief in me. You gotta believe me. I'm sorry. Now what can I do for you … Come on. I'm Peter's partner. Do you want to see my degree?

> *And now* SARAH *is a lawyer. A pretty good one.*

**CONNER & HARRIS:** Yes.

**SARAH:** What is it. The way I'm dressed? I was cleaning up the office. We can't afford a janitor for God's sake. Come on what's the problem. You have some problem with Peter, I take it … Something I can probably help you with.

CONNER: I want him off my back. You think you can arrange that?

SARAH: You're going to have to fill me in here. Peter isn't exactly the most professional of individuals these days. It's his illness, you know. The communication around this office isn't what it should be. He's harassing you. Is that what you're implying.

CONNER: Yeah he's—

HARRIS: I think it's better if we wait for Mr. Maxwell.

SARAH: Okay. But I'm telling you you won't get anywhere with him. He's not behaving rationally.

CONNER: You've noticed that, eh.

SARAH: Well it's hard not to. Come on. Seriously. You can level with me. I was just kidding before. It's late. It's been a hard day. I spent most of it covering up for Peter's lack of judgement.

CONNER *takes* HARRIS *aside.*

CONNER: Obviously she's got a lot in common with the guy. Obviously she knows the guy. She's got a bead on him. Maybe we *can* work this out with her. (*to* SARAH) I'm offering the hand of peace. That's basically what I'm doing. You know me, don't you. You recognize me, I know you do.

HARRIS: Maybe she doesn't.

CONNER: Everybody in this city recognizes me. She lives in this city doesn't she.

HARRIS: Maybe she doesn't.

SARAH: (*to* HARRIS) Whatya mean by that.

HARRIS: Nothing. Maybe you're from out of town … You know from some other place.

SARAH: I used to be from some other place. I'm from here now. I mean I'm trying my best. Come on, give me a chance. I recognize him. He's famous.

CONNER: I wouldn't say famous. I get around though. I make my contributions.

HARRIS: Mr. Conner is the publisher of *The World Today.*

CONNER: She knows that.

SARAH:  Yeah I know that ... That's the paper with all the colour. Lots of blue and red. I like that paper.

CONNER:  You do?

SARAH:  I like it a lot. I read it. I like the way all the articles are surrounded by colour. Borders, I mean. Colourful borders. And the writers, they're interesting. They're mad. They all write like they're really ticked off. I like their angry attitude. I can relate to it.

CONNER:  Do you subscribe.

SARAH:  To what.

CONNER:  To what? The paper.

SARAH:  No. I like it though. I read it on subways. I pick it off the floor. I read it carefully. Then I put it back on the floor before I get off.

CONNER:  People in general like my paper. It gives them what they need. It has balls.

SARAH:  I like balls. Maybe that's why I like your paper. Not the colour at all. The balls.

CONNER:  Yeah.

SARAH:  And a cock.

CONNER:  What.

SARAH:  A cock. Your paper's got a cock. A big cock. That's good. I mean let's stop pretending it doesn't matter ... I know it matters to me. I bet it matters to you too.

CONNER:  Well yeah ... it—

SARAH:  I'm talking about the paper now.

CONNER:  Yeah ... So am I ... I mean—

SARAH:  I like the positions it takes on all the tough issues.

CONNER:  Those are my positions.

SARAH:  I like your positions ... Some people don't. But I do. Your position on downtown development.

CONNER:  I'm for it.

SARAH:  Who isn't for it. Assholes aren't for it. Do I look like an asshole.

CONNER: No you don't. You look unconventional. You act unconventional. But that doesn't make you an asshole.

SARAH: No more than that outfit makes you an asshole. Remember I was just kidding you before.

CONNER: I knew that.

SARAH: Your position on downtown development is closely tied to your position on public housing. Would that be an accurate observation.

CONNER: I think so. Yes ... Wealth leads to wealth. Keep the downtown growing. Eventually there'll be so much money in this city there won't be any need for public housing.

SARAH: Amen to that ... Halfway houses?

CONNER: Pardon.

SARAH: Halfway houses for released prisoners. Mental patients.

CONNER: Now that's a problem.

SARAH: You got a solution?

CONNER: I think I do, ah ... (*snaps his fingers*)

SARAH: Sarah.

CONNER: I think I do, Sarah. I think I've got a solution. I believe we have to protect the vast—

SARAH: No don't tell me. It's probably too complex. I mean there's only so much I can handle at one time. That is unless it's a simple solution. Something real simple. Like killing them.

CONNER: Killing who.

SARAH: The released prisoners. The mental patients. That would work.

CONNER: Sure it would work. But it's not going to happen.

HARRIS: Babe.

CONNER: I mean I don't want it to happen.

SARAH: Me neither. But it would be a simple solution.

HARRIS: Mr. Conner doesn't believe in simple solutions.

CONNER: What are you saying Sean. My whole career is based on offering up simple solutions.

HARRIS: Yes. But not *that* simple. Not solutions *like* that.

CONNER:  Of course not. She knows that.

SARAH:  I was just speculating. Now there's a much maligned word … Speculation!

CONNER:  Oh, God almighty. You're telling me. The whole bloody country is based on speculation. The entire goddamn economy. Everything we eat, we wear, we use. But you hear these people talk about it like it was a mortal sin. These people need a fucking fist down their …

> HARRIS *grabs* CONNER*'s shoulder. Squeezes.*

SARAH:  By 'these people,' I assume you mean people like Mr. Maxwell.

CONNER:  He's your partner. I won't say anything bad about him … to your face.

> CONNER *laughs.* SARAH *laughs.*

SARAH:  Yes that would be awkward. Especially when he has so little time left.

HARRIS:  What do you mean.

SARAH:  A year. Maybe less.

HARRIS:  Are you sure.

SARAH:  You seem concerned. Why is that.

CONNER:  Sean used to be his partner.

SARAH:  Of course. He's mentioned you. I remember now.

CONNER:  What's he say about him.

SARAH:  He says he works for disgusting criminals.

CONNER:  (*laughs*) He works for me!

SARAH:  (*laughs*) He knows that!

CONNER:  Damn that man. That man is misrepresenting me in a very public way. I'm a public man and he's attacking me in a very distressing and personal manner. He doesn't know me. Know what I came from. I came from nowhere. I wasn't born connected like Sean here. I built my connections. I started as a shipper.

HARRIS:  She doesn't want to hear your life story.

SARAH:  I don't mind. (*to* CONNER) Is it a good story. Is it like your paper. Is it angry. Does it have lots of colour.

CONNER: I was born into a working class family. My father was a streetcar driver. My mother—

HARRIS: Look, John. None of that's important at the moment.

CONNER: I was just trying to let her know how hard I—

SARAH: I'm afraid he's right, John. As fascinating as it sounds, it'll have to wait. We've got a problem with Mr. Maxwell that's in desperate need of a simple solution.

HARRIS: Do you have influence with Peter. Can you persuade him, in your own way, to stop his attack on my client here.

SARAH: I can try.

HARRIS: Well that would be good. Because you see Miss—

SARAH: Ms.

HARRIS: Ms. … ah … Sarah … We could all benefit from a reasonable intervention—

SARAH: Look. No need to say more. I know where you're coming from. You're reasonable men. You want a reasonably simple solution. I'll talk to Peter. Whatever he's doing, he's doing it because he's dying. It makes some people bitter. There's no way around that.

CONNER: We could cause him a lot of trouble. If he's dying, he doesn't need any more trouble, does he.

SARAH: Well put. Simply put. Very simply put. Just leave it with me. I'll have my girl call you. Keep you posted.

HARRIS: We could stay. Maybe we should stay and reinforce your arguments.

CONNER: We could do that for you, Sarah.

SARAH: He's a weak old man. I can twist him around my finger.

CONNER: He just hates me. He hates me for reasons I don't understand. It's awful.

SARAH: He's dying Mr. Conner. And you're not. You're in your prime. You've got everything. He's got nothing. Wait a minute. Maybe that's the answer. Give him something.

CONNER: What.

SARAH: Money.

HARRIS: I don't think that's advisable.

**SARAH:** Not in a cheque. Nothing that could be traced. Nothing he could use against you. Cash.

**CONNER:** How much cash.

**SARAH:** How much you got?

> CONNER *takes out his wallet.*

**HARRIS:** My advice on this Babe, would be that—

**CONNER:** She knows the guy. Maybe she's right. Maybe we've blown it out of proportion. Maybe it's just envy. (*to* SARAH) I've got twenty-seven hundred dollars.

**SARAH:** Good. That's good. That's a lot to someone like Petie.

**HARRIS:** He used to spend that much on a raincoat. This won't work.

**CONNER:** It might. Maybe he regrets giving up everything he owns. It's scary down here in the bowels of hell without any resources.

**SARAH:** It's worth a try. Especially when you consider his alternatives. What are his alternatives … I mean, as you see them? (*takes the money*)

**HARRIS:** Unpleasant.

**CONNER:** Yeah. Very unpleasant.

**SARAH:** Hey. Don't get me wrong now, guys. But that sounds like a threat.

> GAIL *comes on.*

**GAIL:** Hi.

**SARAH:** (*to* CONNER) Be with you in a moment. (*goes to* GAIL)

**GAIL:** Where is he.

**SARAH:** (*whispering*) I loved your book by the way. I laughed, I cried. Be with you in a moment. Now where was I. Oh yeah, I was getting money. Petie says to always get money from them. I'll be with you in a moment. (*rushes back to* CONNER *and* HARRIS)

**SARAH:** How much have you got Mr. Harris!

**HARRIS:** Me? This isn't my battle.

**SARAH:** It's a loan. (*to* CONNER) Isn't it. (*to* HARRIS) Your client will pay you back. (*to* CONNER) Won't you.

**CONNER:** Sure. No problem. Give her some money.

**HARRIS:** I don't carry cash.

**SARAH:** I'll take your coat. And your shoes! And your silky silky scarf!! Hand them over. Do it now!

**HARRIS:** What are you talking about.

**SARAH:** Careful now. I've got a witness now. (*to* GAIL) Oh Gail, thank God you're here. They had me backed against a wall. I was terrified. Well look at them. They're terrifying. I think they're with the secret police. Smell them. It's the smell of rancid fascist slime.

**CONNER:** Hey, you're starting up again. I thought you were a reasonable person. (*grabs the money from her*)

**SARAH:** Well that just shows how stupid you are. I'm a mental patient. You've been tricked by a person with a shattered mind. Someone who should just be put out of her misery. I was just playing for time. Waiting for reinforcements. They're here now. Aren't you Gail.

**GAIL:** Yeah. I guess.

**SARAH:** These guys are after Petie. They're hatching vile plots against him.

CONNER *grabs* HARRIS.

**CONNER:** Look, you're my lawyer and I want some answers from you right now! Who is this person and what the hell is she talking about. At first I thought she was wacky. Then she seemed okay. Now she's wacky again. If I had to bet, I'd bet she really is a mental patient. I'm confused by this, so what are you going to do about it.

**HARRIS:** I think we should leave, Babe.

**CONNER:** Good.

*They start off.*

**GAIL:** He called him Babe. Babe's the name of the guy who got Dave sent to prison.

GAIL *is blocking their way to the door.*

**HARRIS:** (*to* CONNER) Who's Dave.

**CONNER:** How the fuck should I know.

**GAIL:** He's my husband. And your goons set him up.

**SARAH:** That right, Babe?

**CONNER:** I don't know what the hell she's talking about.

**GAIL:** Mr. Maxwell has proof.

**HARRIS:** What proof.

> HARRIS *and* CONNER *advance.*

**SARAH:** She's not saying.

> SARAH *grabs* GAIL. *Pushes her out of the way.*

**GAIL:** Yeah. That's right. I'm not.

**CONNER:** Oh you'll say all right

> *He starts to advance on* GAIL.

**HARRIS:** (*grabs* CONNER*'s arm*) Babe. Don't.

> CONNER *throws* HARRIS *off.* HARRIS *falls back onto the couch.*
> CONNER *is still advancing on* GAIL.

**CONNER:** I've taken just about enough shit from you people …
Now what proof are you talking about.

> GAIL *is backing up.*

**SARAH:** Stay away from her.

> SARAH *grabs him. He tosses her off. She lands on* HARRIS.

**CONNER:** Eat shit you crazy bitch. (*to* GAIL) Now what's going on
here. Is this a shakedown. Who are you working for.

> CONNER *is chasing* GAIL *around the desk.* HARRIS *and* SARAH *are
> struggling on the couch.*

**GAIL:** We did nothing to you. We were just minding our own
business. Your two punks threatened my life. A guy named
Moore. A guy named Dawson.

**CONNER:** You've got something connecting me to those men?
What is it. (*suddenly reaches over the desk and grabs her hair*)
What is it!?

> *She bites his hand. He yells. Grabs her in a head lock. Somehow* SARAH
> *is on* HARRIS*' shoulders. Pulling his hair. He is stumbling toward* GAIL
> *and* CONNER. SARAH *yells. Goes from* HARRIS*' shoulders to* CONNER*'s
> back. They start to spin. All four of them with* HARRIS *holding on.*
> *After a few spins,* HARRIS *is thrown off balance. Falls against the wall.*

*Hitting the switch to the conveyor belt. Turning it on.* HARRIS *falls on the conveyor belt, gets his coat stuck. And is going up the conveyor belt, as he yells at the others.*

**HARRIS:** Please! Come on now. Babe, this is something we don't need. Ladies. Please. This is a misunderstanding. We can work this out. We can do better than this!

*SARAH, GAIL, and* CONNER *are a mass of punching, kicking, groaning bodies on the floor by now.*

Please!

*Blackout.*

*Intermission.*

## SCENE FIVE

*Just a few minutes later.*

*The office is a mess. Papers everywhere. A filing cabinet overturned.*
GAIL *is sitting on the floor against the desk.* SARAH *is lying face down near the door.*

**GAIL:** Are you all right.

SARAH *raises her fist.*

I was scared. I was angry. But I was scared too. I think he wanted to kill us. I'm still shaking.

**SARAH:** (*sitting*) I feel good. I got in a few really good whacks. I liked it when I hit him in the nose. I liked the sound. A kind of whomp. Then a kind of whoosh. Whomp. Whoosh. Whompwhoosh. It was satisfying. Maybe I should have started hitting earlier in my life. (*stands*) Honestly. I feel great. I think I might have a broken rib though.

**GAIL:** Seriously?

SARAH *gets on her knees. Crawls over to* GAIL.

**SARAH:** It'll heal. It's a bone. Bones heal.

**GAIL:** Maybe we should take you to a hospital.

**SARAH:** Hospital? No thank you. I usually have a hell of a time getting out once I'm in.

**GAIL:** I've never been in a fight with a guy in a tuxedo before. It was interesting because of that. And he had a lot of cologne on too. Rolling around like that. Ripping away at all that expensive material. Smelling that expensive cologne close up. It was interesting and weird.

**SARAH:** My father smelled good. He smelled 'new.' Always. And he had a lot of nice clothes.

**GAIL:** Was he rich.

**SARAH:** Yeah. And white.

*Pause.*

**GAIL:** Was your mother white.

**SARAH:** Oh yes. She was whiter than my father. She was one of the whitest people on the planet. She was famous in certain circles for it.

GAIL: So ... just you and Eleanor are ... black.

SARAH: Eleanor's not black ... Not really.

GAIL: Oh.

*Pause.*

SARAH: Me neither. Not really ...

GAIL: You just pretend to be black sometimes. Is that right.

SARAH: It helps me get angry. It makes me feel brave.

GAIL: You are brave.

SARAH: No. I'm crazy ... You know ... unrealistic. (*points to her own head. Shakes it. Sadly*)

GAIL: You attacked that guy because I was in trouble. That guy is big. And mean.

SARAH: And in some way crazier than me. I could sense it. He's hearing voices. His voices are ugly. And very confident. I felt a connection to the guy. It wasn't a nice feeling.

GAIL: I felt a rage. I guess that's normal. What he did to Dave. And he's rich. It's normal to feel that about the rich, I guess. My family does. I don't though. Not usually. Usually I don't care. The rich have got their lives. I've got mine. Theirs are better in some ways. Mine's better in other ways. Maybe it evens out. Or maybe it doesn't. Maybe I'm just kidding myself. Maybe that's why I felt the rage. Confusing, isn't it.

SARAH: No. I understand. But that doesn't mean much. Usually the only person I understand is myself. And I don't make any sense.

GAIL: You're making sense now.

SARAH: Did I take a pill. I don't remember. (*takes a small bottle from her pocket*) Did you see me take one of these.

GAIL: No.

*Another bottle.*

SARAH: Or these?

GAIL: No.

*Another bottle.*

SARAH: Or these?

GAIL: No.

**SARAH:** (*stands*) Really. Must have been the fight. It must have been therapeutic. Jesus. Wait till I tell my doctor. 'I don't need the drugs anymore, doc. I just need a good punch-up every once in awhile.' Maybe he'll let me beat up on him. I'd like to. He says he cares. He's supposed to be so dedicated. Maybe he'd let me kick him in the face once a week. Punch his teeth out. Rip his fucking balls off! (*pause*) Sorry.

**GAIL:** That's okay.

> *Pause.*

**SARAH:** I liked your book!

**GAIL:** What book.

**SARAH:** Your story. I read the proofs … Where is it by the way. I put it on the desk.

> GAIL *gets up. Starts to look for it.*

I used to read a lot. I used to know people in publishing. I think I used to be in publishing. Can't remember exactly what I did but it was something fairly important.

> GAIL *finds the pad on the floor behind the desk. Picks it up.*

**GAIL:** It's not a book. It's not a story.

**SARAH:** No trust me. I know about these things for some reason. It's great. You write great. It took me away.

**GAIL:** I was just writing it for Mr. Maxwell. It's supposed to help him with Dave's case.

**SARAH:** It's transcendental. It's gone beyond its initial and common purpose. It's living in the area of a new possibility. It'll make people giddy with sadness. You have to get it published.

**GAIL:** No. It's private. It's my life. I don't think I'd want a lot of strangers reading it.

> ELEANOR *and* MAXWELL *come on.* ELEANOR *is supporting* MAXWELL. *He has his arm over her shoulder.*

**ELEANOR:** Help me. Please.

> GAIL *goes to them.* SARAH *sees* MAXWELL. *Gets scared. Goes into a corner.*

**GAIL:** What's wrong with him.

ELEANOR: I found him collapsed on the steps outside. I think he's having a relapse.

MAXWELL: I'm fine. I just lost my breath.

ELEANOR: Good God! What happened here. Did you do this Sarah. (*to* GAIL) Did she do this.

GAIL: I'll explain later … Why don't we put him on the couch.

MAXWELL: Good plan. A little rest. A little sleep. Even if I slip into a coma for awhile, that's not necessarily a bad thing.

ELEANOR: I'm calling an ambulance.

MAXWELL: No. Please don't. It's not serious.

ELEANOR: Be quiet. You don't know if it's serious or not.

MAXWELL: I think … I just … hypervent— (*stumbles. Falls onto the couch*)

ELEANOR: Enough is enough. I let you move us into this pathetic little hole against my better judgement. But I'm not going to let you die here. (*goes to the desk*) Where's the phone.

SARAH: Doesn't matter. It's broken.

GAIL: It got broken in the fight …

ELEANOR: You two had a fight? Did she attack you.

SARAH: That's your worst fear isn't it Eleanor. When have I ever been violent. Never. (*to* GAIL) Never done a violent thing. But it's her worst fear.

GAIL: She saved me. We were attacked.

ELEANOR: Oh my God. (*to* MAXWELL) Did you hear that. That's what happens when you bring us down to this part of the city—we get attacked! Doped-up strangers break in and attack!

SARAH: Do you think you should be yelling at him at this particular moment, Eleanor.

ELEANOR: Yes!! I'm sorry. But yes! I can't function in this environment! Look at this place. Look at all of you. This place makes me very uneasy. You people make me very uneasy. You people all have problems. They're not my problems. I've got my own.

SARAH: (*to* GAIL) She means me.

ELEANOR: I don't mean you! Yes! Yes I do mean you. You're scaring me to death. You've been scaring me to death for years. (*sits down*) Why don't you just stop it. (*lowers her head*)

> MAXWELL *suddenly sits up.*

MAXWELL: I'm better now! I just hyperventilated. I was so excited by what I found out I just lost control. I started to run. I started to sing. Someone go get Eleanor a glass of water.

SARAH: I'll go. (*leaves*)

MAXWELL: What a mess. Who were they. Did they hurt you.

GAIL: We're fine.

MAXWELL: Looks like you put up quite a fight. You're a tough little cookie aren't you.

GAIL: Not really.

MAXWELL: Of course you are. Who were they.

GAIL: That man named 'Babe' was one. Sarah said the other one was his lawyer.

MAXWELL: Dear dear dear dear dear.

ELEANOR: (*lifts her head*) Sean Harris? Sean Harris attacked you?

GAIL: No. The other one. You see, things got a bit out of control.

> SARAH *comes in with a glass of water.*

SARAH: Yeah. Things just escalated, There was tension in the air. The situation was not healthy. Eventually the situation— escalated. Happens all the time. (*hands* ELEANOR *the water*) Do you want one of my pills, Eleanor. One won't hurt. Here. Decide later when no one's watching.

> ELEANOR *takes the bottle. Puts it on the desk.*

GAIL: It all started because I told Babe we had proof he was connected to those hoods. I don't know why. I was angry. I know we don't have any proof.

MAXWELL: Yes. We do. We have proof coming out the whazoo. Tons of it.

GAIL: Where'd you get it.

ELEANOR: He went for a long walk and made it up.

**MAXWELL:** No. I was willing to do that. I was capable of taking that route. But I decided to do some legitimate investigation first. Usually I disdain investigation. It gives due process a respect it doesn't deserve. But, well the truth is I wanted to know if I was still mentally capable of following one piece of information logically to another and making reasonable deductions along the way.

**SARAH:** What's that like. It sounds boring.

**MAXWELL:** Well it's like a strong narrative in a book. It can be pleasant enough. But it's not really necessary if—

**GAIL:** So what have you got?

**MAXWELL:** Pictures. Would you believe it. Lovely little pictures. You see, the bad guys like to have their pictures taken with big shots. They keep scrap albums apparently. The big shots don't know about it. But it goes on. Apparently it's a real underworld trend. Life is just great when it surprises you like this.

**GAIL:** So you've got pictures of Babe Conner with the hoods, is that right.

**MAXWELL:** Yes it is.

**ELEANOR:** Can I see them.

**MAXWELL:** Sure.

> MAXWELL *reaches into his pocket. Takes out a large envelope. Hands it to her.* ELEANOR *looks inside the envelope.*

**ELEANOR:** Where did you get these.

**MAXWELL:** I bought them.

**ELEANOR:** You bought them?

**MAXWELL:** Yes! I went undercover. I followed information. I found a source. I made a purchase. Two hundred dollars and worth a million times that.

**ELEANOR:** Where did you get two hundred dollars. You don't have any money. Neither of us has any money. We're working for free these days, remember!

**MAXWELL:** Well, I don't know how I got it. I just reached in my pocket and it was there. It was a spiritual moment. I almost swooned.

**GAIL:** So what do we do now.

**MAXWELL:** Well now we explore our options. There are several.

**ELEANOR:** Here's one I think might be appropriate. Call the police.

**MAXWELL:** I'm sorry. I'd like to. Just for your sake Eleanor if for no other reason. I know you still have a reservoir of faith in the veneer of civilization. But I can't. The police are encumbered by their role within the system. The system is the thing which caused the turmoil in the first place.

**SARAH:** What's he talking about. I love what he's saying. But what does it have to do with anything I could do.

**GAIL:** He's talking about getting Dave out of prison.

**ELEANOR:** No he's not.

> GAIL *throws her hands up in the air.*

**MAXWELL:** You're right. Dave's just part of it. What we have here is a focal point in the struggle. An historical watershed. A convergence of apparently random injustices. And it is our duty—*our* duty—to take this moment and amplify its significance until it reverberates to a point where the walls come tumbling down. The walls which surround the privileged and the self-righteous, the walls which … which— (*grabs his head*) Oooh that's a bit scary … I'll be honest now … It's pain.

> ELEANOR *grabs his arm.*

**ELEANOR:** Okay, that's it! You're going to a hospital.

> MAXWELL *falls to the floor.*

**MAXWELL:** No. When the time comes … I want to skip the hospital and go directly to the morgue.

**SARAH:** I can relate to that. Get rid of the middleman.

**ELEANOR:** Hyperventilation. You were lying. Admit it. (*trying to pick him up*)

**MAXWELL:** I was just thinking positively.

**ELEANOR:** You're having another stroke. I can't allow you to die here.

**MAXWELL:** I want to die here. (*frees himself from* ELEANOR)

**SARAH:** (*looking scared*) He wants to *die* here.

> SARAH *goes into a corner.*

**MAXWELL:** I don't mean to be rude but it *is* my death after all. And I'd rather go through it without tubes and wires.

**ELEANOR:** (*looks at* SARAH *and* GAIL) Isn't anyone going to help me convince him.

**SARAH:** Don't look at me. I don't get that 'will-to-live' stuff in the first place. I'd like to inject us all with enough pure heroin to put us permanently out of our misery within minutes … That's a lie.

**GAIL:** I think he's right, Eleanor. My father died in the hospital. They kept him alive with all those things. It didn't make anyone very happy. He wasn't happy. My mother wasn't happy either.

> MAXWELL *is rocking back and forth. Holding his head.* SARAH *turns toward them tentatively.*

**SARAH:** Besides, maybe he's all right. Why don't we just think of him as being all right. You know, just think him back to health.

**MAXWELL:** Yeah. That's a plan I like. Oooh. Pain pain pain.

**ELEANOR:** It's not working, is it.

**SARAH:** I haven't started yet. Let's have a little faith here Eleanor.

**ELEANOR:** Do you think I want him to suffer. Don't you think I care. I've worked for this man for fifteen years.

**GAIL:** Try it Eleanor. What have you got to lose. Just concentrate. Think about him being all right … Tell yourself he's doing just fine.

**SARAH:** Yeah. It's that easy. Concentrate.

> *And* SARAH *closes her eyes. Concentrates. Hard.*

**MAXWELL:** I think … they may be on to something here.

**ELEANOR:** Who are you people. How did you find one another. Were you given maps at birth. Did God bring you together. Do you share some mysterious ailment.

**MAXWELL:** I think it's working.

**ELEANOR:** Is it a virus.

**SARAH:** I think he looks better.

**ELEANOR:** Why am I immune.

**MAXWELL:** It's definitely working.

**GAIL:** He's definitely better. It's amazing. It's exciting too.

**MAXWELL:** I think I'm going to be all right.

**GAIL:** Sarah. Look at him. He's better. It worked.

**SARAH:** No thanks to any of you. I said concentrate, not talk. I was stranded out there on the primal plane all alone. Petie, did you feel me zapping you with those positive negative ions.

**MAXWELL:** I think so.

**ELEANOR:** Honestly now Peter, how do you feel. Don't pretend just to humour her.

**SARAH:** Oh right! The guy's going to fake recovery from brain implosion just so he won't hurt my feelings. And she thinks I've got a problem with reality.

**MAXWELL:** I'm going to stand. Aren't I, Sarah.

**SARAH:** Yes!

> SARAH *gets behind him. Helps him stand.*

**MAXWELL:** I'm standing up! I'm going to walk. Aren't I, Sarah.

**SARAH:** Yes!

> SARAH *starts walking with* MAXWELL. *Holding him up from behind.*

**MAXWELL:** I'm walking!

**SARAH:** There was a time when this sort of thing would have been considered a miracle. Not that I want the publicity, but shouldn't we call someone.

**MAXWELL:** Let's see how long it lasts first.

**ELEANOR:** Is the pain gone.

**MAXWELL:** We won't use the word pain anymore. Let's forget about pain for the time being. Okay everyone? Now we've got to get moving here. There seems to be something about the dynamic of this particular group that keeps us from focusing properly. But we've got to overcome that. Time is a precious commodity. Okay … Gail.

**GAIL:** Yes, Mr. Maxwell.

**MAXWELL:** Did you see Dave today.

**GAIL:** Yes I did.

**MAXWELL:** And he gave you the names of those two guys.

**GAIL:** Yes. And where they live.

**MAXWELL:** God that's good news. News like that can make a man live forever. (*breathes in and out a few times*) Man I feel great. Really great. Okay. Eleanor.

**ELEANOR:** Yes Peter.

**MAXWELL:** Did you get all that stuff on Babe Conner from the library.

**ELEANOR:** Everything they had.

**MAXWELL:** Which was plenty.

**ELEANOR:** Yes.

**MAXWELL:** Yes. Because he's a high profile man. A contributor. An investor in the future. But I've looked through the hole in my head and seen his idea of the future. It's a nasty stupid place. Okay! We've got to swing into action. Gail and Sarah come with me. Eleanor, you stay here.

**ELEANOR:** And do what.

**SARAH:** Tidy up. (*to* MAXWELL) She loves to tidy up. She's brilliant at it. Gets it from our mother.

**ELEANOR:** And what will the rest of you be doing if you don't mind me asking.

**MAXWELL:** Changing the world. Our little part of it. Don't feel left out though. It's a big job. We'll need all the help we can get. You'll be included.

**ELEANOR:** I'm grateful. Honestly.

**MAXWELL:** Can we take your car, Eleanor.

**ELEANOR:** Oh certainly. I'd be honoured. The keys are on my desk.

> GAIL *and* SARAH *help* MAXWELL *to the door. He has an arm over each of their shoulders.*

**SARAH:** This is an adventure isn't it. We're going somewhere. To do something. That's an adventure.

**MAXWELL:** Yes it is.

**GAIL:** Is it dangerous.

**MAXWELL:** Yes it is. But don't worry. You'll do fine. You're a tough little cookie.

**GAIL:** Not really.

**ELEANOR:** Sarah stays.

**SARAH:** Sarah goes. (*leaves*)

**ELEANOR:** Peter ... Peter ... Peter!

**GAIL:** (*to* MAXWELL) We'll wait for you in the car.

> GAIL *leaves. Pause.* MAXWELL *is leaning against the frame of the door for support. He looks at* ELEANOR.

**MAXWELL:** Don't be mad at me. It's just a little adventure. I mean I've got to do something to keep their spirits up. We should dedicate our new lives to people like Sarah and Gail. The troubled and marginal. You know ... those people.

**ELEANOR:** 'Those people' trust you, Peter.

**MAXWELL:** I know. And I'm sincerely moved by that. Their trust gives me strength.

> ELEANOR *holds up the envelope.*

**ELEANOR:** These are fake. You had these pictures of Mr. Conner with the two criminals made up. They're fakes. And they're not even good ones.

**MAXWELL:** They can be improved. The guy at the lab says any composite needs to go through a few touch-up phases.

**ELEANOR:** So you're actually planning to use them.

**MAXWELL:** Of course.

**ELEANOR:** That's a criminal act.

**MAXWELL:** I don't care.

> ELEANOR *gets his cane. Hands it to him.*

**ELEANOR:** Here.

**MAXWELL:** Thanks.

> *He leaves.* ELEANOR *sighs. Starts to pick things up. Sighs. Takes some rubber cleaning gloves from her pocket. Puts them on. Picks up a bottle of cleaner from a corner somewhere. Looks at it. Sighs. Puts it down. Picks up the glass of water. And the bottle of pills. Goes to the couch. Looks at the pills.*
>
> *Blackout.*

## SCENE SIX

*Later.*

*ELEANOR is asleep on the couch. The office is still a mess. Suddenly the conveyor is humming. And a large body wrapped in a pink drape is coming down on it from the street. MAXWELL, SARAH, and GAIL come rushing in. Get to the conveyor as the body reaches the bottom. One of them hits the switch. It stops. They start to lift the body.*

**MAXWELL:** Careful. Don't drop him.

**SARAH:** I've been trying to drop him all the way from the car.

**GAIL:** Is that why you tried to trip me out on the street.

**SARAH:** Yeah. Sorry.

**MAXWELL:** Let's put him in that chair.

*There is a chair next to the desk. They aim for it.*

**SARAH:** Wow. This is one beefy white guy we got here. If the economy collapses and we're reduced to the worst possible scenario, the meat on this guy could feed us all for a year.

**GAIL:** Sarah.

**SARAH:** Just a passing thought. I mean, come on. Am I the only person who thinks about cannibalism from time to time. I doubt it!

*They have the body in the chair.*

**MAXWELL:** What's Eleanor doing.

**GAIL:** Sleeping. It's three in the morning, Mr. Maxwell.

**MAXWELL:** Really? I've lost track … Look at her. I've never seen her asleep before. She looks so placid. I think she'd like us to wake her up though. I'm sure she'd want to be part of this.

**SARAH:** I don't.

**GAIL:** Me neither.

*SARAH is picking up a pill bottle from the floor near ELEANOR's outstretched hand.*

**SARAH:** Besides, there's no waking her anyway. She took a couple of my pills. These things are lethal.

**GAIL:** Does that mean she's going to die.

**SARAH:** I meant lethal in the figurative sense … whatever that means.

**GAIL:** Does it mean she's just in a deep sleep.

**SARAH:** Ah, yes. It does. Thank you.

**MAXWELL:** Why do you suppose she took pills, Sarah.

**SARAH:** I don't know. And until she changes her attitude to just about everything in the world, me included, I'm not sure I care.

**GAIL:** What do we do with him.

**MAXWELL:** I thought I told you what we're going to do with him.

**GAIL:** I meant for now. Should we … unwrap him.

**SARAH:** I'm against that. Unless we cover up his eyes. His eyes are invitations to hell. He shot me a look while we were attacking him that turned my blood to ice. This is one beefy *evil* white guy we got here … Leave him in his drape. It looks good. I like the colour. Pink is a very calming colour, did you know that. I wonder why a guy like this would have pink drapes. Why would he want to get calm.

**MAXWELL:** Maybe it helps him think.

**GAIL:** Think about really shitty stuff. Think about getting innocent kids to do his dirty work for him. Ruining their lives. God I hate him. I want to kick him. I really do.

**SARAH:** Go ahead.

**MAXWELL:** You don't have to kick him. You have other options now. You can bludgeon him with accountability.

**GAIL:** When.

**MAXWELL:** Soon.

**GAIL:** How soon.

> HARRIS *comes on. In a trench coat. Under the trench coat, jogging pants and sweatshirt.*

**HARRIS:** All right, Peter. What was that phone call all about. What's all this about.

**MAXWELL:** (*to* GAIL) Starting now.

**HARRIS:** You can't just call people at two in the morning with a bunch of veiled threats and think— (*points at body*) What's that.

MAXWELL: (*to* GAIL) Uncover him.

> GAIL *starts to unwrap the body.*

SARAH: Everything except his eyes.

MAXWELL: No. He has to see. It's only fair. We're not barbarians.

SARAH: Okay. But if he shoots me a look I can't be responsible for my actions.

HARRIS: Is that who I think it is.

MAXWELL: Yes.

HARRIS: What did you do. Kidnap him?

MAXWELL: Yes.

HARRIS: Well you've done it now. There's no way out of this one, Peter. I'm getting the police.

> SARAH *rushes over. Blocks the door.* HARRIS *backs away from her.* GAIL *has* CONNER*'s head uncovered now. And is struggling to get the drape off his body.* CONNER *is unconscious. His mouth taped. His head drooping.*

Jesus. Look at him. Is he dead. Oh my God. (*points to* ELEANOR) Look at her. Is *she* dead. What is going on here. Are you people on some kind of rampage.

GAIL: Yes.

MAXWELL: Sean. (*takes a step toward* HARRIS) Let me explain. There's a way out of this for everyone.

HARRIS: Stay away from me. Why would you want to kill me, Peter. I've never done anything to you. All right so I've got your family. But you can have them back. Sandra, the kids, all of them. All right, so we don't agree politically anymore. But politics is compromise. We can work it out. If I'm elected I'll keep a—what's that thing? ... Open mind. You and your friends will always have my ear. Listen. I'll even defend you. I'll go the stress route. Have it reduced to manslaughter. I know Conner probably drove you to it ... I don't know what Eleanor did to you but I'm sure it was hideous. Hideous.

MAXWELL: Shut up! Calm down. Come on, calm down. No one's dead. Eleanor's just having a little nap. And we had to drug your friend Mr. Conner. It was the only way we could get him to come with us.

HARRIS: Drug him? Where'd you get the drugs.

SARAH *giggles.*

From her?

**SARAH:**  Yes. I've got lots of them. Needles too. I'm an entirely self-contained pharmaceutical factory.

**HARRIS:**  You're a dope addict. I told Babe you were a dope addict. That's the only reason we didn't press charges against you for attacking him. We felt sorry for you ... I felt sorry for you too Peter. Reduced to practising law with junkies ...

**MAXWELL:**  Does anyone know what he's talking about.

**SARAH:**  I do. But I'm not telling.

**HARRIS:**  I'm getting out of here. Everyone stand back. I'm waking up Babe. And we're both leaving. Do you understand me. I'm being firm now ... If you don't cause any more trouble we might not call the police. We'll see how you do in the next few minutes.

**MAXWELL:**  Sit down, Sean!

SARAH *and* GAIL *help* HARRIS *into a chair.*

The police are out of the question. We're not going that route. And when I'm finished explaining to you, I don't believe you'll want us to either. How did your announcement go. Were people enthusiastic. What do the early polls show. Do they look good? I bet they do, you old smoothy you. (*to others*) This guy's going to get elected. Does anyone in this room have a problem believing that.

**GAIL:**  I don't.

**SARAH:**  The self-destructive part of me would vote for him. The socially conscious part of me would vote against him. But the part of me I personally like the best, the part that believes in primal justice, would throw him to the floor, rip off his clothes and pour battery acid down his rectum.

MAXWELL *goes to* SARAH. *Touches her head. They nod at each other momentarily.* MAXWELL *then turns back to* HARRIS.

**MAXWELL:**  Well ... Well I wouldn't vote for him. I wouldn't elect him to anything. He's a greedy prick. Aren't you, Sean.

**HARRIS:**  Depends on your point of view I suppose.

**MAXWELL:**  Come on admit it. You've admitted it to me before. Joked and laughed about it in locker rooms many times.

**HARRIS:** All right. I'm a greedy prick. So what.

**MAXWELL:** Exactly. No I wouldn't vote for him. But thousands will. Well he just ... looks ... so damn good. I'd say he's a shoe-in. Unless of course, there's a ripple. (*points to* CONNER) He could be your ripple, Sean. Don't say I didn't warn you.

**HARRIS:** What are you talking about.

**MAXWELL:** He's a crook. (*to* GAIL) Isn't he.

**GAIL:** Yes.

**MAXWELL:** We've got proof (*to* SARAH) Haven't we.

**SARAH:** Yes.

**MAXWELL:** He's a proven crook. And he's your crook. Just like you're his candidate. There was a picture in the paper of you together at your announcement. Hands clasped. Arms raised. It was a lovely picture. It made me feel great. When I saw it I knew I had you.

**HARRIS:** How.

**MAXWELL:** That picture bonds the two of you in the public's eye.

**HARRIS:** What do you want from me, Peter.

**MAXWELL:** The first thing is this. We want you out of politics. We don't want you running this country Sean. You're a greedy prick. And maybe that's all right for you and your friends, but hey, they're greedy pricks too. And we've already got enough of them to deal with. So you're not going to seek public office. Do you agree to that.

**HARRIS:** No, I don't.

**MAXWELL:** You must want it very badly. That makes me feel great. I'll tell you why in a minute. Second thing is, we want you to get Gail's husband out of prison.

**HARRIS:** Why. Is he important to you for some reason.

**GAIL:** He's innocent.

**HARRIS:** (*laughs*) Sure he is.

GAIL *advances on him.*

**HARRIS:** No. Sure. He is!

**MAXWELL:** Listen to her Sean. Personally, I've decided to restrict the word innocent to descriptions of angels and newborn babies. Let's just say he's not guilty of the crime for which he was convicted.

**GAIL:** Conner's guys, his thugs, sent Dave into one of the other newspaper's warehouses. To smash up some machinery. They sent him into another one's office to steal some advertising information or something. They told him if he didn't do it, they'd come after *me* and hurt *me*.

**MAXWELL:** In our newly revised way of looking at things, the law included, that makes Dave not guilty. Get him out. I don't care how. Get him an appeal. Use your connections. Or have Conner get his thugs to confess. Like I said I don't care. Just get it done. We'll be monitoring your progress on this, Sean.

**HARRIS:** First I want to know what you have connecting Mr. Conner to these alleged criminals.

**MAXWELL:** Pictures.

**HARRIS:** Okay. I want to see them.

**MAXWELL:** No you don't. You know I've got them. You know me well enough to know I wouldn't enter into the fray unprepared. I mean I'm a new man, Sean. But some old habits are worth keeping.

**HARRIS:** Well, nevertheless it could be difficult. These things take a certain amount—

**MAXWELL:** We're off that subject, Sean. We're moving on. (*to* GAIL) How's Mr. Conner.

**GAIL:** He's coming to.

> GAIL *rips the tape from* CONNER*'s mouth.* SARAH *takes a rope from her knapsack. Begins to tie* CONNER *to his chair.*

**MAXWELL:** What we want you to do now is the big test. If you do it well we could resolve this dilemma without anyone getting seriously hurt. Without your reputation getting seriously hurt. And therefore any chance you have of getting elected. Do you understand.

**HARRIS:** Yes.

**MAXWELL:** Good boy. But you'll have to do your best. No sloughing off. None of that famous disdain for the fanciful they've all grown to love at your club.

**HARRIS:** Yes, yes. What is it.

**MAXWELL:** A trial.

**HARRIS:** A what.

**MAXWELL:** A trial.

**HARRIS:** Whose trial.

> MAXWELL *points at* CONNER.

**MAXWELL:** His.

**HARRIS:** For what. For those break-ins?

**MAXWELL:** No no. That's small potatoes. We can live with our earlier resolution to that injustice. This is bigger. More … more …

**SARAH:** Cosmic. In an urban sense.

**MAXWELL:** Yes. And also more satisfying. He is going to stand trial for his newspaper, for his public stands on all the major issues of the day, on his contributions to making this city a place which is only satisfying to baseball fans and real estate agents! For his endless manipulative use of the lowest common denominator and his lack of respect for the essential mysteries of life!

**SARAH:** The official charge is: Being … Consciously … Evil.

**MAXWELL:** (*to* HARRIS) And you are defending him. It's a simple win-lose situation. If we win he closes his newspaper. If you win, we don't go public with proof that your friend is a low-life crook.

**GAIL:** But he still has to get Dave out no matter what.

**MAXWELL:** That's a given.

**SARAH:** Let's get started.

> GAIL *and* SARAH *start to tidy up a bit. Move the desk more centre. And rearrange the chairs.* CONNER *stirs. Moans. In a daze.*

**CONNER:** Hey. Where am I.

**GAIL:** In court.

**SARAH:** On trial for your life.

**HARRIS:** His life? What does she mean by that.

**MAXWELL:** She was probably speaking figuratively. She often does … Were you speaking figuratively Sarah.

**SARAH:** No I was trying to scare the shit out of him. I don't like him.

**MAXWELL:** You see, Sean? Just an honest expression of simple human feelings.

**GAIL:** (*to* MAXWELL) How are you feeling, Mr. Maxwell.

**MAXWELL:** I'll get through it. Maybe I should just sit down for a moment though. Get prepared. (*sits on the couch*)

**HARRIS:** Surely you don't seriously expect me to go along with this, Peter.

**MAXWELL:** I'm sorry, but you don't have a choice. I warned you to break your ties to this guy. And now your reputation is at stake. And because you're a man without a soul, your reputation is the only thing you have. Relax. All you have to do is win. Winning is second nature to you.

**HARRIS:** Of all the demented, screwed up, hare-brained, pathetic, half-baked ideas. A trial. A goddamn trial!? Who are you. God? No. You're nothing. You're a sick old man with delusions of grandeur. You're pitiful. You're living the life of a fool. You're surrounded by fools. Pathetic. Why are you doing this to me. Why? Because I'm a greedy prick? You were a greedy prick too. For twenty years you were one of the greediest and one of the biggest!

**MAXWELL:** I repented.

> HARRIS *sits on the couch next to* MAXWELL. *They have to roll the sleeping* ELEANOR *on her side to make room.*

**HARRIS:** You can't. You can't repent just like that. That's not how it works. Even I know that.

**MAXWELL:** Yes you can. You just say to yourself 'I repent.' You send a message out to the world that you're sorry for what you've been. Any kind of message.

**HARRIS:** Okay. I repent too.

**MAXWELL:** Too late!

**HARRIS:** Says who.

**MAXWELL:** (*standing*) Me! Me! The demigod. The former greedy prick. The man with a hole in his brain. The angry man. The reborn man. The avenger! I warned you didn't I ... The avenger is here. And it's me!!

**HARRIS:** Come on. Get a hold of yourself. It's not too late to stop—

**MAXWELL:** Shut up! (*smiles*) I'm preparing. I'd advise you to do the same, Sean. I'd advise you to get deadly serious about this right now! Confer with your client if you wish.

CONNER *stirs again.*

**CONNER:** Hey. Is this a dream.

**SARAH:** Yeah. And it's beautiful.

SARAH *is staring off into the distance.*

**MAXWELL:** Everyone take a minute. Gather your thoughts. This is a monumental task we're about to undertake.

**GAIL:** Yeah. I feel like praying or something.

**MAXWELL:** Good idea. Everyone look inside your head. Locate your individual God. Have a few words.

CONNER *stands. Notices that he is still tied to the chair.*

**CONNER:** Jesus Christ!

**SARAH:** Typical choice.

*Blackout.*

## SCENE SEVEN

*A moment or two later.*

*The basic courtroom set-up.* SARAH *is the judge. She is sitting behind the desk. Wearing the pink drape around her shoulders. In front, and to one side of her,* GAIL *is taking notes, as the court stenographer.* ELEANOR *is still asleep on the couch.*

*Down to the right of the desk a chair for* MAXWELL. *Down and to the left two chairs—one for* HARRIS, *one for* CONNER, *who is still tied to the chair. And is gagged again.*

*The scene begins in darkness. Except for a light on* SARAH. *Yelling.*

**SARAH:** Order. Order. Order in the court. I'll have order. Give it to me. I want it. It's mine! Orderrrrr!

*Lights up on an argument. Both* HARRIS *and* MAXWELL *are leaning on the desk.* SARAH *is on her feet.*

**HARRIS:** There are no rules here! Where are the rules!

**MAXWELL:** To hell with the rules! We don't need—

**HARRIS:** This is anarchy! I can't work this way.

**SARAH:** Order! (*to* HARRIS) You. Sit down or I'll have you put in handcuffs. What are you doing here anyway.

**HARRIS:** I'm the lawyer for the defendant!

**SARAH:** That's the spirit! (*smiles*) Just checking. (*to* MAXWELL) He's committed. We can proceed. You're out of order too by the way. Sit down.

**HARRIS:** What's she going on about. When did the trial begin. Who made her judge. See what I mean? No rules!

**MAXWELL:** Wing it. Speak from the heart, man.

**HARRIS:** Well what's the framework. Common law?

**MAXWELL:** Let's not be parochial. We've got choices you know. Even within the common law. British, Canadian, American.

**SARAH:** The only trials I've seen have been on TV.

**MAXWELL:** It'll have to be American then.

**SARAH:** We'll make it up. We'll do fine. Just be nice boys. Try to get along. (*to* GAIL) Are you getting all this.

**GAIL:** You're going too fast.

**SARAH:** Don't write it down verbatim. Just aim for the essence. You're a born writer, honey. Just do your thing.

**MAXWELL:** And remember you're writing for posterity. Don't worry about the structure. But use lots of imagery. (*to* HARRIS) That okay with you?

**HARRIS:** I want my client ungagged.

**SARAH:** We tried that. But he started to talk. What he said made the court nauseous. He'll be allowed to testify on his own behalf.

**HARRIS:** That's big of you.

**SARAH:** That's big of you, what.

**HARRIS:** I don't know. What!?

**SARAH:** That's big of you, *Your Honour.* You watch it now. I'll hold you in contempt. And you don't want to know what being held in contempt means in my court. Got that?

**HARRIS:** Yes ... your honour.

**SARAH:** Good boy. (*to* MAXWELL) Present your case.

**MAXWELL:** Thank you, Your Honour. On behalf of the people I wish to—

**HARRIS:** I ... He ... I mean ... Objection, Your *Honour.* He has no right to claim he represents the people. Who are the people. The people here? An amorphous mass outside ... I mean come on—

**MAXWELL:** I use the term 'the people' quite correctly, Your Honour. Societal crimes have been committed and the victims of these crimes are in fact—

**SARAH:** Yeah yeah. Objection overruled. (*to* HARRIS) Calm down. It's just a word. People. I can relate to what he means. Don't worry. This court isn't too crazy about 'the people' anyway. He doesn't get any advantage saying shit like that around me. (*to* MAXWELL) Continue. No wait. Something's wrong. I think I should be higher. In a position to look down on you all. I think the looking down thing is essential here. (*grabs a waste can. Puts it on the desk. Sits on it*) This feels better. (*to* GAIL) How's it look.

**GAIL:** I just wrote that you look like a primitive warrior. A kind of furious but wise queen. Like someone in the Bible.

**SARAH:** She's a genius. (*to* MAXWELL) Well, what are you waiting for. Speak.

**MAXWELL:** We will attempt to prove that the accused, knowingly and with total disregard for the consequences, pursued a career injurious to the public well-being. That he—

**HARRIS:** Objection. That's impossible to prove.

**SARAH:** Well why not let him be the judge of that. It's his job after all.

**HARRIS:** Very well. It's impossible to defend against.

**SARAH:** Try. Maybe you'll surprise yourself.

**HARRIS:** So what you're getting at here, Peter—what upsets you—if you'll allow me to put it in terms that a mere mortal like myself—someone not in touch With God's true purpose on earth—can understand, is that you don't like the choice of headlines in the guy's newspaper. You don't like—what?— his view of the world, or something.

**MAXWELL:** Oh for God's sake. I don't *like* butterscotch ice cream. I don't *like* people who only talk seriously about foreign films. This guy, this buddy of yours is an enemy of the human race. So what I'm *getting* at, what *upsets* me about his newspaper is that it promotes the theory of the survival of the fittest. The law of the jungle. And the problem with that is actually very simple to understand. This is not a jungle! It's a civilization! Get it? Get the difference? Well your buddy doesn't, or for some very cynical reason he chooses not to. And that is why I *despise* him from the bottom of my soul.

**HARRIS:** Yes, but what has he *done*?! What has he actually done that he has to defend himself. To anyone. To any court. Even to this sorry excuse for a court.

**SARAH:** Be careful.

**MAXWELL:** You heard the charge.

**HARRIS:** Being evil? What's that mean. That's purely subjective.

**MAXWELL:** No, it's a matter of consensus.

**HARRIS:** But how are you going to prove it!

**MAXWELL:** Well just watch me, you silly bastard!

**HARRIS:** I'd like a moment to confer with my client.

**SARAH:** Go ahead. But be quick about it.

**HARRIS:** Don't push me! I can only be pushed so far!

**SARAH:** You think so? Well I'll push your asshole through your brain until you're inside out in another fucking universe! The Universe of the brainless assholes! Don't ever fucking tell me how far I can push someone! It's bad for my fucking health! Bad for everyone's fucking health! It's bad therapy! Bad karma! Bad fucking manners!!

**HARRIS:** Oh please. Help me out here Peter. I can't deal with her at all. I can't. I just ... fucking can't!

**MAXWELL:** Just talk to your client if you're going to talk to him! I haven't got all day, man!

HARRIS *goes over to* CONNER. *Whispers to him.* CONNER *begins to nod.*

**GAIL:** How are you feeling, Mr. Maxwell.

**MAXWELL:** To be honest ... Not great.

**GAIL:** You look a bit pale.

**MAXWELL:** Headache. A pretty bad one. And I think it's growing. I wish he'd hurry up over there. I don't know how much time I've got. Come on, Sean!

**HARRIS:** I wish to make a suggestion ... Your *Honour*. I think we should skip the opening ... statements. I've talked to my client and he agrees to testify at this point in time. He also promises not to make any undue fuss. This way Mr. Maxwell here can proceed with direct interrogation and I will have a recognizable structure to operate within. Agreed?

**SARAH:** Agreed.

**MAXWELL:** Agreed.

HARRIS *starts to untie* CONNER. ELEANOR *stands up. Stretches.*

**ELEANOR:** Oh well that was a sleep to remember. Those pills are something— (*looks around*) What are you doing up there, Sarah! Please get down. (*to others*) Has there been an incident. I'm so sorry.

**SARAH:** Hey. I didn't do anything wrong. Just go back to sleep. Everything is fine.

**MAXWELL:** Come over here, Eleanor. Take my chair.

*She does.*

**ELEANOR:** What's going on.

**SARAH:** Just do what he says. Listen. Watch. You might learn something.

**MAXWELL:** (*helping her into the chair*) I might need you to assist me. I'm not feeling that—

**ELEANOR:** Why. What's wrong with you.

> CONNER *is free. He attacks* MAXWELL.

**CONNER:** Okay. What's stopping me from pounding the shit out of all of you right now.

**MAXWELL:** (*to* HARRIS) I thought you explained to him!

> HARRIS *pulls* CONNER *off* MAXWELL.

**HARRIS:** I did. (*to* CONNER) Take the stand, Babe. We've both got too much at stake here.

**CONNER:** Oh I'll take the stand all right. I'll take the stand and wrap it around this asshole's skull. Then I'll take the pieces and ram them down the throat of that crazy bitch up there.

**HARRIS:** This won't help, Babe. Like I told you they have—

**CONNER:** Yeah I know. They've got some proof about some little thing. But shit. They broke into my house. They attacked me. They put needles in my arm. They threw me in the trunk of a car. This is some kind of fucking nightmare. What did I ever do to these people. And I have to take this shit? I have to sit down and take this abuse from these people. Why. I'm asking you why.

**HARRIS:** I told you why!

**CONNER:** I know! But it doesn't seem like enough of a reason. It's like I want a better reason. It's almost like I want to ask God for a reason. I feel that fucked up about this thing. Jesus! I'm a citizen of some standing in this community.

**MAXWELL:** You're a thieving, conniving, merciless, exploiting piece of sewage!

**CONNER:** I am not!

**MAXWELL:** Prove it!

**HARRIS & CONNER:** How!

**SARAH & MAXWELL:** Take the stand!

**CONNER:** Yeah. Okay. Okay yeah. I'll take it. Where is it. I'll take it. Then you'll see. I'm not afraid. Jesus. Where is the fucking *stand!*

**SARAH:** That chair down there. Next to me.

> CONNER *goes to chair. Sits. Weeps.*

**CONNER:** (*to* HARRIS) Did you hear the names that guy called me. They were horrible. Just rotten. (*looks up*) God. It's me. Sorry to bother you. But what's goin' on here.

**ELEANOR:** (*to* MAXWELL) Is this what I think it is, Peter.

**MAXWELL:** A trial. Yes.

**ELEANOR:** Oh dear.

> ELEANOR *stands.* MAXWELL *sits.*

**HARRIS:** (*to* SARAH) I suppose you want to swear him in, in your own inimitable fashion.

**SARAH:** Yeah. (*to* CONNER) You're going to be asked some questions. Are you going to lie.

**CONNER:** No!

**SARAH:** Oh sure. We really believe that.

**HARRIS:** That's prejudicial. I want another judge.

**CONNER:** So do I.

**SARAH:** I was just expressing my true feelings. I think it best if the court is honest about these things. It doesn't mean I can't be turned around or anything. You guys have forgotten almost all the important things about life haven't you.

**HARRIS:** Make Eleanor the judge. She's a fair person.

**SARAH:** (*mocking*) 'Make Eleanor the judge. Make Eleanor the judge.' 'She's fair. She's coherent. She's neat. She's normal.' No way. It ain't gonna happen. I'm here. And I'm staying. You hear that Eleanor? So stop promoting yourself for my job. (*starts to cry*) Just stop it!

**ELEANOR:** I don't want the job, Sarah. Believe me.

**SARAH:** Oh you're lobbying for it all right. Standing there the way you do. Standing there all rational. And deferential. Looking perfect for the position. Just waiting for the chance to serve.

> *The next three speeches come simultaneously.*

**ELEANOR:** Don't Sarah. You're getting yourself all worked up. It just won't do, so stop it!

**GAIL:** Leave her alone. She's a good judge. She's doing just fine.

**MAXWELL:** Please, my head. Please! Sarah's the judge!

*Pause.*

**CONNER:** (*looking up*) Are you hearing all this God. This is the thanks I get for being a good citizen? Making my contribution? Providing over three hundred jobs? This is my reward? Putting my fate in the hands of these lunatics? Oh man I'm confused by this. I'm right on the edge here. (*drops to his knees, closes his eyes, begins to pray*) Oh Lord. Give me your wisdom here. Pass it along, Lord. Help me defeat my enemies. Help me find my way back into the light. Help me stay prosperous and productive. Dear Jesus. Help me crush these assholes. Help me to—

*About halfway into* CONNER's *prayer,* ELEANOR *advances and stands above him silently. Now she quickly takes off her rubber cleaning gloves and begins to slap* CONNER *with them.* CONNER *hides behind* HARRIS. *And* ELEANOR *is slapping them both.*

Hey! Hey what the fuck. Jesus ... Hey ...

**ELEANOR:** How dare you talk to God like that! How dare you ask God to save your miserable hide. You leave God out of this. The nerve of you asking him to keep you prosperous when there's so much real pain in the world! (*starts back to her chair*)

**CONNER:** (*jumping up*) Okay. That's enough. She hit me. She's gonna die! (*starts after her*)

*SARAH throws off the drape and jumps on his back.* GAIL *jumps and puts a head lock on him.* HARRIS *and* MAXWELL *join in to separate them. They form a mass of bodies and collapse on the couch in a tangle.*

**HARRIS:** No! No no. Not again. Come on now.

**MAXWELL:** Sarah. Gail. This isn't the way.

**HARRIS:** Get them off him.

**MAXWELL:** I'm trying. Help me. Please!

*They are all groaning. Talking. Finally* CONNER *gets free. Stands. The rest of them are on the couch. Except* ELEANOR *who remains in her chair. Looking worried. And angry.*

**CONNER:** This is what I mean. This is the perfect defense. Where do you people get the right to judge anyone. You're a bunch of screw-ups. You've got me on your own terrain. You've taken away all my rights. Taken me away from a world where I have status. And you still can't pull it off. You're pathetic!

**ELEANOR:** No they're not! They're just struggling. Struggling to replace a ... a ... system that has let them down for some reason. Be nice to them! They're only looking for a little justice.

CONNER *goes to* ELEANOR.

**CONNER:** I've done nothing wrong! I didn't know those punks were going to pull that rough stuff. I was engaged in a little industrial espionage. It gets done to me all the time.

**ELEANOR:** Well at least now you're admitting it. Did you hear that, Peter. He's admitting it.

**CONNER:** What's the point of denying it. He's got pictures of me with those two bozos hasn't he.

**ELEANOR:** Yes he has. And don't you forget it!

**CONNER:** What's the fuss. It's just a little crime. It happens all the time. Everyone does it. It's part of the game. Part of the real world.

SARAH *stands.*

**SARAH:** Real to who? It's not real to me. It's an obscene fantasy to me. People managing and arranging. People being managed and getting arranged. Just thinking about it makes me want to vomit.

HARRIS *stands.*

**HARRIS:** We don't care how you feel about it. You're not capable of taking part in it. You're obviously a very ill person. I feel sorry for you. It's because I feel sorry for you that I'm willing to subsidize your medical expenses.

**CONNER:** (*to* SARAH) Subsidize! Yeah. I hire celebrities to entertain people like you in the hospital. My ex-wife is a fundraiser for that hospital. She does it because she cares and because I pay her alimony, she's got the time to care. I love this country. I love this city. My contributions to this city are legendary. I support the opera.

**HARRIS:**  So do I.

> SARAH *is between them. Looking at each in turn. Wide-eyed.*
> *Incredulous.*

**CONNER:**  I support the United Appeal.

**HARRIS:**  So do I.

**CONNER:**  I support the Boy Scouts, the Girl Guides and three day care centres. I sponsor a little league team, two bantam hockey leagues.

**HARRIS:**  I sponsor one of those too.

**CONNER:**  I promote the building of sports facilities in this city. Sports are very important. They help keep people healthy.

**HARRIS:**  People who want to be healthy. People who aren't afraid to meet life head on.

**CONNER:**  People who want to be successful.

**HARRIS:**  You bet.

> *And now* CONNER *and* HARRIS *talking only to each other. Joyfully.*
> *Passionately.*

**CONNER:**  Successful on the right terms.

**HARRIS:**  The terms of a true consensus. They're the foundation of our society, those people and their consensus. It's a prosperous society. Deny that.

**CONNER:**  No way. I can't.

**HARRIS:**  I mean compare it to any other society. Sure there are people who get left out. That's a pity. There are people living on the street. But overall—

**CONNER:**  Fuck the people living on the fucking street. I've heard enough about the fucking people on the street. I mean you'd think there were thousands of them, the kind of press they get. I mean Jesus man this has got to be a place for winners. We've got to keep the momentum going. Let the slower people pick up the jet stream. That's our only choice. We've got to get richer. The only alternative is to get poorer.

**HARRIS:**  I love this man! (*points at* CONNER) This is a brave man.

**CONNER:**  Thank you.

> *They hug. They pat each other on the back. They're on the verge of tears.*

**HARRIS:** No. Thank you. Thank you for your courage and your contributions. And your spunky little newspaper that gives people what they need. And thank you for hiring me. And getting your friends to hire me. And helping me stay rich. (*stands on the desk*) And thereby allowing me to run for public office and thereby helping me help everyone else become rich. (*to others*) Rich is good.

> CONNER *buries his head in* HARRIS' *crotch.*

It's good. It's very very good!

> *A noise up on the street. Garbage cans rattling.* MAXWELL *stands. Starts toward the window.*

**MAXWELL:** Hey you! I've told you not to eat that garbage! (*to others*) They won't stop. I've asked. I've pleaded ... They just won't stop!

**SARAH:** Time for the verdict. Guilty. Both of them. I sentence them to death by drowning. In the toilet. Let's get them down to the washroom.

**CONNER:** Back off!

**SARAH:** You back off!

**CONNER:** I mean it!

**SARAH:** He means it! I'll fucking show you what meaning it means.

> *She advances quickly on* CONNER.

**MAXWELL:** Stop it, just stop it! Get them out of my sight. They won. I lost my fire. I'm sorry, okay! I think I'm dying.

> ELEANOR *and* GAIL *go to* MAXWELL. *Help him into a chair.*

**SARAH:** All right. (*to* HARRIS) If he says so—you won.

**CONNER:** We know. We could feel it. We recognized the feeling, didn't we Sean.

**HARRIS:** Definitely.

**SARAH:** Don't push your luck. I'm letting you go out of respect for a dying man. A man I love.

**HARRIS:** No police, Peter? No press? Nothing about the break-ins?

**ELEANOR:** Hey. He's a man of his word. You should at least know that!

**GAIL:** Just make sure you get my husband out of prison.

**SARAH:** We'll be monitoring you.

**ELEANOR:** Remember, we've still got those pictures. And they're great pictures.

**HARRIS:** Come on, Babe.

> HARRIS *picks up the pink drape. Puts it around* CONNER'*s shoulders.*

**CONNER:** Sure ... So this was just an argument right ... I mean if you leave out the rough stuff. Kind of ... a debate. And we beat the crap out them. Looking back it was kind of exciting.

> *They start off.*

**GAIL:** There's something I'd like to add to the argument.

> *They turn. Look at her. Laugh. Start off again.* GAIL *takes a small gun from her pocket. Fires it in the air. They stop.*

**CONNER:** (*turns*) Jesus.

**HARRIS:** What's this. Peter, what's she doing.

**MAXWELL:** Gail.

**ELEANOR:** Please. Not a gun. Anything but a gun. (*to* MAXWELL) Ask her why she has a gun.

**GAIL:** The first time I met this guy, he attacked me remember. I wasn't going to be in a room with him again without any protection. It's not that I didn't believe in you Mr. Maxwell. I've just learned to be prepared.

**HARRIS:** So what do you want.

**GAIL:** Like I said. I just wanted to add something to the argument.

**CONNER:** Yeah, what?

> GAIL *holds up the gun.*

**GAIL:** This. It's real.

**HARRIS:** We know.

**GAIL:** You see I've been listening ... Mr. Maxwell didn't lose his fire. He's just a gentle man at heart. Or maybe he's just forgetful. Anyway he left something out of the argument. And this is it. The gun. See it? If you cross me or my husband again, I'll use it. If you make me mad again I'll find you and put it against your head and pull the trigger. Maybe because I

think you're wrong about all the things you talked about.
Maybe for ... some other reasons. We'll never know for sure
why I use it. I'll never know because I'll be too busy getting
on with my life to ask myself questions like that. And you'll
never know because you'll be dead ...

HARRIS *and* CONNER *look at each other.*

**HARRIS:** Well you've really ticked her off.

**CONNER:** And I don't even know who she is ... Anyway she was
talking to both of us.

**HARRIS:** No way.

**CONNER:** Ask her.

**HARRIS:** I don't want to.

**GAIL:** Hey ... You can leave now.

*They turn. Leave.*

**ELEANOR:** Gail. Where did you get that gun.

**SARAH:** I gave it to her ... I've had it for quite awhile. Just in
case.

**ELEANOR:** Just in case what.

**SARAH:** Just in case I had to use it ... You know? Use it? (*uses her
fingers as a gun, puts it to her head, pulls the trigger*)

**ELEANOR:** Oh my God.

**GAIL:** What's it matter how I got it. I've just got it. And those
guys know I've got it.

MAXWELL *stands.*

**MAXWELL:** Gail. It's an honour to have known you. (*to others*) She
is your leader. Follow her to the promised—

*He collapses into* ELEANOR*'s arms. She sinks to her knees.*

Eleanor, is my will on file. I want to bequeath some money to
Sarah and Gail.

**ELEANOR:** You don't have any money, Peter. You gave it all away,
remember.

**MAXWELL:** Ah yes. (*to* SARAH *and* GAIL) Well I was thinking of
you. Trust me. It really is the thought ... that counts ...
Eleanor, you look like my mother.

SARAH *is backing away.*

**ELEANOR:**  You never told me that.

**MAXWELL:**  You never looked like her before ... Until just ... this moment.

**SARAH:**  I don't know why he's talking like this. Or why he looks the way he does. Am I supposed to be worried here. I don't feel very well.

**MAXWELL:**  Sarah. Come here.

**SARAH:**  No. I can't.

**MAXWELL:**  Please.

> SARAH *is rubbing the floor with one foot.*

**SARAH:**  No. I'm ... I'm ... doing something. I'm very busy here at the moment. Maybe later. We'll talk. Have lunch or something ... I don't know.

**MAXWELL:**  She's scared.

**ELEANOR:**  Who isn't.

**MAXWELL:**  Oh Lord. I've let you all down haven't I.

**ELEANOR:**  Yes.

**GAIL:**  No.

**ELEANOR:**  I'm sorry. I meant to say no. Honestly. You did fine Peter. You had those men very very scared there for awhile.

**MAXWELL:**  Didn't want to ... scare them. Wanted to dazzle them. Turn them inside out. I was naive, right?

**ELEANOR:**  Yes.

**GAIL:**  No.

**ELEANOR:**  Yes. Damn it! Yes. Naive! Unbelievably dangerously naive! ... I'm sorry ...

**MAXWELL:**  It's all right. in some cases naive is preferable ... But not this time. I left it too late. My rebirth. Tried to ... cram it all in ... I should have started earlier. When I was younger ... spread the anger out a ... bit.

> *He dies.* ELEANOR *lays him down gently.*

**SARAH:**  What are you doing. Don't put him down on the floor like that.

**ELEANOR:**  He's dead.

**SARAH:**  Who says.

**ELEANOR:** He stopped breathing.

**SARAH:** Well maybe he'll start again.

**ELEANOR:** Sarah.

**SARAH:** Don't start. I don't want to hear any of your coherent talk, Eleanor. Just pick up his head. Hold it for awhile. Cradle it. Give the guy a chance to reconsider. Maybe he's just weighing his options. Show him you love him Eleanor. Maybe he'll come back to us. Why do you give up so easily, Eleanor. Why won't you just pick up the poor guy's head.

**ELEANOR:** (*to* GAIL) Can you help me explain to her.

**GAIL:** Pick up his head, Eleanor. What have you got to lose. It might make you feel good ...

ELEANOR *sighs. Lifts* MAXWELL*'s head. Puts it in her lap.*

**SARAH:** Massage his head a bit. Really gently. Gently. Gently.

**ELEANOR:** How long do you want me to do this, Sarah.

**SARAH:** I don't know, For as long as it takes I guess. I've never brought anyone back from the dead before. It could take hours. Weeks ... I think he's worth it though. Worth the effort ... (*to* GAIL) Don't you.

**GAIL:** Yes.

**SARAH:** I mean the guy had something. He was on to something. (*to* GAIL) Don't you think?

**GAIL:** Yes. I do.

**ELEANOR:** I can't keep doing this, Sarah. It's wrong. It's making me feel so—

**SARAH:** I need him Eleanor. I need him back. He created an environment that was good for me. He made a connection in my head. His anger connected to my anger. It blotted out the voices.

GAIL *puts her hand on* SARAH*'s shoulder.*

**GAIL:** I can do that. I can do that for you.

**SARAH:** Yeah?

**GAIL:** Yeah ... I think so.

**SARAH:** So ... well ... what can I do for you.

**GAIL:**  You're great. It's just great to be around you. We'll just be friends. It'll be exciting for me. You're the most amazing person I've ever met.

**SARAH:**  Yeah? You hear that Eleanor?

**ELEANOR:**  Yes.

**SARAH:**  We're going to be friends. (*to* GAIL) You're not saying all this just because we're the same colour, are you.

**GAIL:**  No.

**SARAH:**  You hear that, Eleanor? She and I are really going to be friends. And it's going to be exciting. What do you think of that.

**ELEANOR:**  I don't know.

**SARAH:**  Well at least she's not against it.

> ELEANOR *and* GAIL *look at* SARAH. *Then all three look down at* MAXWELL*'s body. Concentrate.*
>
> *Lights fade to black.*
>
> *End.*

# *Tough!*

*Tough!* was first produced by Green Thumb Theatre for Young People. It opened at the Vancouver East Cultural Centre on February 4, 1993 with the following cast:

TINA   Robyn Stevan
BOBBY   Frank Zotter
JILL   Leslie Jones

Director: Patrick McDonald
Set & Costume Designer: Phillip Tidd
Lighting Designer: Gerald King
Stage Manager: Cynthia Burtinshaw

*Persons*
**TINA**, nineteen
**BOBBY**, nineteen
**JILL**, nineteen

*Place*
A city park.

*Time*
Now.

# Tough!

*Early evening. Late summer. A small city park. A picnic table. A trash can.* BOBBY *is sitting on the picnic table, watching* TINA *move around in a very agitated way.* JILL *is lying on the grass a few feet away, writing something on a thick pad.*

BOBBY *is wearing a work shirt, jeans, and boots.* JILL *is wearing a t-shirt and jeans.* TINA *is wearing slacks and a nice blouse. She is carrying her shoes.*

**TINA:** It's all lies. Everything you ever told me was a fucking lie. You said I could trust you. That's a lie. You let me think I knew you. What did I know about you. Lies. I knew your lies. Ah shit, aren't you going to say anything. Are you just gonna sit there like a dog. A lying dog.

**BOBBY:** So what do you want me—

**TINA:** Shut the fuck up. Anything you say now is gonna be a lie.

**BOBBY:** No, it's not.

**TINA:** No? You're gonna say something truthful? Why? Why start now. Cause you're under pressure?

**BOBBY:** I'm not under pressure. There's no pressure. I could leave, you know. I don't have to stay here and listen to this stuff.

**TINA:** You could leave and I'd follow you. You could run and hide and I'd track you down like the sad animal you are. And grab you by your fucking ears. And yell the truth into your sad stupid lying face. And I will, you know. I will. So you know you gotta sit there and take it. Because you deserve it. You're a shit. A real shit. And you know what else you are? You're a coward. What. What?! You wanna say something now? You getting mad? You don't like being called a coward, coward. Well what?! What?!

**BOBBY:** You want me to talk?

**TINA:** You wanna talk? Talk. Who's stopping you.

**BOBBY:** Ah ... Listen ... Okay. All I want ... I mean the only thing now is that maybe you're making too much out of what—

**TINA:** Jesus! You had your hand up her shirt. You had your hand up her fucking shirt.

**BOBBY:** Yeah, that's the story. That's what's going round. But—

JILL *sits up.*

**JILL:** Hey! I saw you, asshole.

**BOBBY:** This is a set-up. I was brought here under false circumstances.

**JILL:** False circumstances. What the hell does that mean. Talk English.

**BOBBY:** It's like a trial. You never liked me.

**JILL:** You're right. But what's that got to do with anything. I still saw you take that bimbo slut into the kitchen.

**BOBBY:** (*to* TINA) See? Okay, that's not true. Not really. She took me. Really. I was—

**TINA:** Look, be careful. You're gonna lie. You're gonna lie and then I'm gonna kill you.

**BOBBY:** Fuck it. It's a trial. You've got a witness who never liked me. She's the only one giving testimony so I'm fucked ... It's like you've set a trap for me or something. Like you think I'm an animal or something.

**TINA:** I *do* think you're an animal. I've already told you that.

**BOBBY:** Well, I'm not.

**TINA:** Prove it. Explain to me that you've got some human reason for what you did. Because a human would have a reason and an animal would just have done it because it's what an animal does.

**BOBBY:** Come on. I've been working all day. I can't deal with this now. My mind's all fuzzy.

**TINA:** I've been working all day too and my mind's sharp as a tack.

**BOBBY:** Yeah well, that's one of the ways we're different.

**TINA:** Breasts.

**BOBBY:** What.

**TINA:** Tits. That's what it's about. Nothing else.

**BOBBY:** Ah, come on.

**TINA:** Tits, man. You're like a kid. You're ... you know ... What's the word.

**JILL:** Obsessed.

**TINA:** Yeah. Right. Obsessed. You're obsessed with tits. It doesn't even matter what they're attached to. They could be attached to a fence and you'd still go after them. Tits just glued to a fence and you'd be in there rubbing against them. Feeling up that fence, man. People would be stopping and watching. 'What's that guy doin' to that fence.' You wouldn't care. You'd be drooling away, whispering to that fence, 'Can I suck them. I really wanna suck them.'

**BOBBY:** Look, it was a party. I was drinking. I wasn't clear in my head.

**JILL:** Oh, right. Excuse me while I lie down and ignore this. (*she does*)

**BOBBY:** (*to* JILL) You had to tell her, eh.

**JILL:** Well, I thought about it all weekend. I weighed the pros and the cons. But then, yeah, I had to tell her.

**TINA:** (*to* BOBBY) Betrayal. Do you know what that word means.

**BOBBY:** I was trying to tell you how drunk I was. I was ... really drunk.

**TINA:** No, you have to shut up. You can't go down that road. It's not gonna work. Suppose I told you I was drunk when I agreed to go out with you that first time.

**BOBBY:** Were you.

**TINA:** Jesus. It was an example ... A thing you use. What's wrong with you. Are you stupid. Did I make that mistake about you too. I thought you had a brain in your head.

**BOBBY:** What's the deal. You just get to insult me until you feel better, or what.

**TINA:** You were planning to do it with that mindless slut. Don't deny it. Just tell me why. I just want to know why.

**BOBBY:** I was—

**TINA:** You can't say you were drunk. I'll kill you if you say that.

**JILL:**  I'll help her.

**BOBBY:**  I want her to leave.

**JILL:**  Tough.

**TINA:**  Yeah, that's right. Tough.

**BOBBY:**  She's done her thing. She's given her testimony. Why can't she just ... go away ... I can't deal with this in front of her.

**TINA:**  She's here for me. I don't care how you feel about it.

**BOBBY:**  (*stands*) Okay. So *I'll* leave.

**TINA:**  You leave, we're finished. Got it? You leave, fuck you.

**BOBBY:**  Why are you swearing so much. You hardly ever swear. You have a bad day at work? Look, I told you that job could be rough. Selling jewellery is dicey. What do you know about jewellery. I warned you.

**TINA:**  (*to* JILL) Are you listening to this.

**JILL:**  Unbelievable.

**BOBBY:**  (*to* JILL) Hey, I know she's upset with me. I'm just saying she's so upset it's gotta maybe be a combination of things. I mean, swearing and threatening my life, it's outta whack with the ... you know, the thing I did ... So I'm just saying—

**TINA:**  You ripped out my heart! You diseased brain-damaged sewer rat! You killed me! I thought we were in this for life. That was one of your lies. You said forever.

**BOBBY:**  Forever. Jesus.

**TINA:**  What.

**BOBBY:**  Forever. I mean, come on.

  *She moves to him.*

**TINA:**  What.

**BOBBY:**  Forever is ... What's that mean. I mean, come on. I'm really very young. I've got a whole life to live.

**TINA:**  Wrong!

  *She swings really hard and hits him on the side of the head. He howls. Rolls off the table.*

  (*to* JILL) I'm outta here.

**JILL:**  I'm right behind you.

TINA *leaves.* JILL *gets up. Brushes herself off. Looks at* BOBBY *who is now on one knee. Rubbing his head.*

**BOBBY:** What. You wanna hit me too?

**JILL:** Hit you? No. I was thinking I should have brought my knife. I told Tina. Let's bring a knife and cut off his balls.

**BOBBY:** Wow. What's your problem. How come you hate me so much. What did I ever do to you. It's weird the way you hate me so much. It really bothers me.

**JILL:** You've been messing around for months haven't you. This was just the first time you were caught. Right?

**BOBBY:** I'm not saying anything. What can I say. This is a trap. You're setting me up. Ah, this sucks. I've been working like a dog all day. My life isn't exactly great, you know. I've got problems no one knows about. Heavy ones. Confusing too. Confusing heavy problems about ... life. I'm not an animal to be trapped. I'm a guy with problems. Jesus.

**JILL:** Stop whining. I've got something to tell you.

**BOBBY:** I've got enough to deal with without you telling me anything.

**JILL:** She's pregnant, asshole. Deal with that.

*Pause.*

**BOBBY:** Tina? Pregnant? ... Pregnant ... Pregnant ... Pregnant?

**JILL:** What. You tryin' to figure out how to spell it or something.

**BOBBY:** Pregnant?

**JILL:** Yes. Yes! Pregnant. Carrying a baby.

**BOBBY:** No way. No sir.

**JILL:** Carrying your baby.

**BOBBY:** No way. No no no no no. Hey, come on. Me? No way. No.

**JILL:** You little insect. Are you denying it. Are you gonna try and weasel out of this.

TINA *comes running on.*

**TINA:** (*to* BOBBY) You fucking coward. (*to* JILL) I heard him. I was hiding behind a tree. I knew he'd deny it. And he did. (*to* BOBBY) Coward! If I had a gun I'd shoot you. What's happened to you, Bobby. You used to be a human being.

**JILL:**  He was never human. He was always an insect in disguise. You were just blinded by love.

**TINA:**  Killed by love. Run over and flattened by love. I'm dead. Really. My life's over. Ah, what am I gonna do.

> *She starts to cry.* JILL *hugs her. Sound of a siren going by on the street near them. This immediately takes* BOBBY's *attention.*

**JILL:**  Don't cry in front of him. Don't let him see this.

**TINA:**  I can't help it. It's the way I feel.

**JILL:**  Try to feel something else. Think about getting revenge or something. I liked it better when you talked about getting a gun. Say something else like that.

**TINA:**  No! I just wanna be sad. Can't I be sad here. Aren't you my friend. Can't you just let me be whatever way I have to be. Can't you.

**JILL:**  Yeah. I guess. Yeah, go ahead. Cry. (*to* BOBBY) Are you happy now. Look at her. Hey! Try to pay attention. What's wrong with you. (*to* TINA) God I can't believe you've let a guy like this into your life. I really don't think crying in front of a guy like this is a good idea.

**TINA:**  I can't help it … He denied it. I really … never thought he'd deny it. I said I thought he would … But I didn't really think he would.

**BOBBY:**  (*stands suddenly*) I use condoms! Always! Condoms are my thing. I was using them before anyone. I use them all the time. Ask … anyone.

**TINA:**  I can't talk to him until he admits it's his. Can't he see what he's saying about me by not admitting it's his.

**JILL:**  Sure he's saying you're as much of a betraying cowardly whore as he is. He knows that.

**BOBBY:**  But I use condoms! She knows I use condoms.

**JILL:**  You have to stop saying that. (*pats* TINA. *Walks over to* BOBBY) You have to stop talking about condoms. (*grabs* BOBBY *with both her hands by his shirt*) Get it?! Because you're talking about them like they're some kind of gift from God or something. Some powerful thing that God gave you to make you immune. God didn't give you the condoms, asshole. You bought them in a store. The store bought them from a company that's got a factory. The factory makes them. And sometimes the factory fucks up ... Everyone else on the planet knows this. I gotta think you know this too and you're just looking for a way out of this mess. But there isn't one. There's no way out. You're the father of this baby and if you don't just admit it pretty damn soon we're going to kill you. We're going to kick you to death. Okay?! ... Okay?!

BOBBY: Yeah, but—

JILL: But nothing! You're the father of this child. My friend Tina does not sleep around. *She only sleeps with you!* Because she *loves you.* Don't ask me why. I don't know. No one knows. None of her friends know. Her mother doesn't know. I bet God doesn't even know. It's a mystery of the universe that even God doesn't fucking understand!

BOBBY: I'm ... not feeling very well. Please let me go. You've said your thing. I ... just need to be let go now.

JILL: You gonna run away? Running won't work, I'm telling you.

BOBBY: No. I'm not running. I can't run. I'm sick. I just need some ... You're too close. I can't breathe. Please let me go. Please.

TINA: Let him go. He's pretty pale. He passes out when he's that pale. I've seen it.

JILL: I don't like you, Bobby.

BOBBY: I know ... Please, just let me go. Okay? ... Okay?

JILL: Yeah ... Okay.

> *She lets go of him. He goes to the picnic table. Sits.*

BOBBY: (*to* JILL) Thanks.

TINA: Put your head down. Between your legs.

BOBBY: Yeah. (*he does*)

TINA: (*to* JILL) He's got a condition. A kind of anemia. Had it since he was a kid. He's got to take shots.

JILL: I didn't know that.

TINA: I think I told you once.

JILL: I never listened when you were talking about him. I pretended to. Just to be polite, you know.

TINA: Oh.

**JILL:**  I mean I listened when it had to do with you. Your feelings and stuff. But things that were just about him, I zoned out. You gotta remember I've known this guy just about all my life. Longer than you. Since kindergarten. And I've never seen anything in him that I like.

**TINA:**  Not even a little?

**JILL:**  No.

**TINA:**  Come on. There must have been something. A little thing.

**JILL:**  No, not really.

**TINA:**  That's strange, eh. Because usually we like the same things. I mean more than usually, really. Almost always.

**JILL:**  I remember when I found out you were going together. I remember saying to myself, 'You gotta warn her about him.'

**TINA:**  Why didn't you.

**JILL:**  I did. I told you every selfish rotten thing I could remember him doing.

**TINA:**  Love is blind.

**JILL:**  And deaf

**TINA:**  And stupid. And you know what else love is? Love is dangerous. I'll never love again. It's too dangerous. If I live through this I'm going into seclusion. Even at work. I'll ask them to take me off the counter and move me into the store room. I can do inventory. You hardly have to see anyone doing inventory … How you feeling, Bobby.

**BOBBY:**  Who cares.

**TINA:**  Keep your head down. You look awful.

**BOBBY:**  I never understood why she didn't like me.

**TINA:**  Who.

**BOBBY:**  Her. Jill. I mean, what's so bad about me. Compared to other people. She's hated me since we were five years old. It's … just … weird.

**TINA:**  Keep your head down.

**BOBBY:**  Well, she said she wanted to kick me to death. I think it's weird. I don't know …

**TINA:**  She just wants you to take responsibility.

**BOBBY:** Everything's in my face … and rushing into my head. You know? All of a sudden I'm a rotten shit. Some rotten little shitty thing that people want to kick to death … I'm just trying to tie things together for myself. I'm really very young and things— (*shrugs. Gestures. Shakes his head and lowers it*)

**TINA:** What.

**BOBBY:** I've got things to say. But I can't say them in front of her. What's she doing here anyway. And what's she writing. I mean is she taking notes or something.

**TINA:** What are you writing, Jill.

**JILL:** It's an essay.

**BOBBY:** Yeah, right. School hasn't even started.

**JILL:** It's a multi-purpose essay. I know what courses I'm taking. It'll fit in somewhere. Maybe twice, even.

**BOBBY:** Well, great. I've got all these hard things to say to you and your friend the university student is just gonna lie there and write an essay.

**TINA:** What kind of things.

**BOBBY:** Things to … things to just say to you, I guess. You're pregnant. So … well … okay. Right. Okay. So I … need to … what I need to say about that … I don't know. Ah, fuck it. She can stay. What's the difference.

**TINA:** No, she'll go. You can go, Jill. Is that okay.

**JILL:** Is it okay with you.

**TINA:** Yeah. I guess.

**JILL:** You're sure?

**TINA:** Yeah. You can go … But …

**JILL:** What.

**TINA:** Not home. Can you just go for a walk. Don't leave altogether I mean. I don't know. Maybe … you could just wait over by that tree.

**JILL:** Ah. No. Bad idea. Hookers hang around trees. Some guy will take me for a hooker. Come up to me. Piss me off. I'll have to kill him … How about I go over to the store. Get something. A Coke or something.

**TINA:** Yeah. And then come back.

**BOBBY:** She doesn't have to come back. I'll walk you home if that's what you're worried about.

**TINA:** Maybe I won't want you to walk me home, Bobby. There's no guarantee.

**JILL:** You want a Coke?

**TINA:** Sure.

**JILL:** What about him. Should I get him a Coke.

**TINA:** You want a Coke, Bobby?

**BOBBY:** She doesn't want to get me one.

**TINA:** She offered.

**BOBBY:** Yeah, but she doesn't really want to. I don't know why she offered. Probably so she could say something crappy to me if I said yes. Something like 'Get it yourself!'

**JILL:** Ah, for chrissake. You want a Coke or not?

**BOBBY:** Diet Coke.

**JILL:** Diet Coke. (*laughs*) Jesus … See ya. (*leaves*)

**BOBBY:** See? Just cause I wanted a Diet Coke, she makes a thing about it. She laughs that way she does. She's been laughing at me like that since we were five years old. Shit, I'm haunted by her. It's like she knows something about me even I don't know. Something really rotten, I guess … What is it. Do you know what it is she knows that I … don't.

**TINA:** Bobby. This isn't—

**BOBBY:** No, it's all tied together. I think it is. It's a feeling I've got. Her attitude towards me has something to do with my attitude towards myself or something. And that's gotta have something to do with why I'm not … you know, myself really. I mean my better self. I mean myself really about you and … you know … it … If it, you know, the … I mean I'm not saying you're lying but are you sure you're …

**TINA:** I'm sure. I went to a doctor.

**BOBBY:** And he was sure.

**TINA:** She. Yes. It's due in February.

**BOBBY:** Ah, Jesus … Ahhh … Jesus … (*puts his head between his legs*)

**TINA:** Are you all right.

BOBBY: Am I all right ... Am I all right ... No. No, I'm not all right. Definitely not. I'm scared shitless. (*gets up. Starts to pace*) Come on. Come on, get a hold of yourself, Bobby. Come on, man. (*stops suddenly*) Shit. That's right. You're right. I'm a coward. Holy fuck. How'd you know that. She told you, didn't she. Jill told you. That's the thing she knows. And she told you. And she's right. I'm a fucking coward. Holy fuck. I don't even care about you I'm so scared. I want to, I want to care about you. But really I don't. Holy fuck. I'm scum!

TINA: Is this a trick.

BOBBY: What.

TINA: What are you pulling. Am I supposed to feel sorry for you.

BOBBY: Hey, look. I'm scum. I'm just telling you.

TINA: I think it's a trick.

BOBBY: It just came to me. Whatya mean a trick.

TINA: If it's not a trick what is it.

BOBBY: It's nothing. It's what I am. I'm just telling you.

TINA: Why.

BOBBY: Whatya mean why. It just came to me.

TINA: I think you think it's a way out. You tell me you're scum, cowardly scum, and I just write you off. Let you off the hook. Is that what you're doing.

BOBBY: I don't think so.

TINA: Whatya mean you don't think so.

BOBBY: Well, if I'm real scum I'd pull anything wouldn't I. I might not even know what I was pulling. I'd just be doing it because that's the way a scum works. I mean a scum would want off the hook, there's no doubt about that.

TINA: You prick! I can't believe I'm even listening to this. What is this garbage. We're not going down this road. Forget it. What do you think I am. Some martyr or something. You think I'll just write you off and take it all on my shoulders. Say to myself 'Bad choice, Tina. He was just a mistake. Well, live and learn. On with my life.' No way. What kind of scum would pretend to be a scum. Jesus ...

**BOBBY:**  Look. I'm under pressure. I'm not sure I'm saying what my head isn't— Look, okay. I had plans. I was going to go back to school. I didn't tell you that, I know. But I was talking to my dad.

**TINA:**  Shut up. The hell with you. What about me. And the baby. What about the baby.

**BOBBY:**  The baby?

**TINA:**  The baby. The baby!

**BOBBY:**  Wow. It's not a baby yet. Don't call it a baby. You'll get attached to it.

**TINA:**  Whatya mean by that. I said whatya mean.

**BOBBY:**  Nothing. I don't know.

**TINA:**  Abortion. You're thinking abortion.

**BOBBY:**  I'm not thinking anything.

**TINA:**  Liar. You are.

**BOBBY:**  I'm not. I'm not thinking anything. And anything I'm thinking I'm not understanding. Come on. Give me a break.

**TINA:**  Go to hell. Go away. I've changed my mind and I want you out of my sight. That's what you wanted. You got it. Piss off.

**BOBBY:**  Wait a minute.

**TINA:**  Wait for what.

**BOBBY:**  A minute. I never said—

**TINA:**  All that cowardly scum talk. That's what you wanted.

**BOBBY:**  I was thinking out loud. You know, trying to … trying to understand my … you know, feelings. I've got … you know, feelings too. I was just trying to understand them.

**TINA:**  Yeah, right.

**BOBBY:**  No, really. I felt like scum so I started thinking I *was* scum. I mean I was feeling bad anyway. Feeling bad about …

**TINA:**  What.

**BOBBY:**  The thing. The thing that happened at the party … in Jill's kitchen. I mean we never really talked about that.

**TINA:**  You wanna talk about it now?

**BOBBY:**  Not really. But I was feeling bad about that. And you and Jill were in my face about that. I'm not blaming you but …

Anyway. So I felt like scum. And then I thought if you feel like scum, maybe you *are* scum. And then she tells me you're pregnant. Wham! (*hits himself on the head*) Wham wham wham! But anyway ... Well, I don't want to go. I want to ... you know stay here with you. Look, I just want to sit down for a minute. And figure out what I want to say to you. I know I want to say something. I just need to figure out what it is.

*He looks at her. She shrugs. Sits next to him. Pause.*

My jacket.

**TINA:** What?

**BOBBY:** Where's my jacket. I thought I brought it.

**TINA:** I don't think so.

**BOBBY:** I need a smoke. I think they're in my jacket.

**TINA:** Are you gonna say you want to go home and get your jacket.

**BOBBY:** That wouldn't be a good idea?

**TINA:** Not really.

**BOBBY:** Okay. Well ... But I need a smoke.

**TINA:** Yeah, you need a smoke. Maybe you need a drink too. Maybe you need to take some heavy drugs. Maybe you need to meet a rich girl with big breasts and live in a condo in Hawaii for the rest of your life. Tough. You're here. What you've got is what you've got. Now if you've got something to say to me say it.

**BOBBY:** I'm going to.

**TINA:** When.

**BOBBY:** Now.

*Pause.*

**TINA:** Hey, Bobby. Now is like ... now. Now isn't soon. It's right away.

**BOBBY:** Yeah but—

**TINA:** Speak!

**BOBBY:** Speak? Speak ... Speak.

**TINA:** Speak! Tell me about us. And the baby. How it's going to be. What we're going to do! What do you want to do!

**BOBBY:** I don't know what I want to do. I only know what I was going to do! I was ... going to break up with you.

*They are just looking at each other.*

**TINA:** Yeah?

**BOBBY:** I ... was going to break up with you. I had that in my mind. It's been coming. It was in the back of my mind and then ... it was in the front.

**TINA:** Yeah?

**BOBBY:** For a few weeks.

**TINA:** For a few weeks? Really.

**BOBBY:** Because ... because, well, I've been looking around, you know. I found myself looking around at ... others ... and thinking, hey, they look nice. Why can't I be ... with them too. I mean look at the way they dress, it's nice.

**TINA:** I can't believe you're telling me this.

**BOBBY:** Me either.

**TINA:** I mean you're making me sick.

**BOBBY:** Sure. Me too. It's sickening. I was sick about it. I've been sick about it for months.

**TINA:** Months? Now it's months.

**BOBBY:** Maybe not months. Weeks. A month ... and a half maybe.

**TINA:** You've wanted to be with other people for a month and a half?

**BOBBY:** But I was sick about it. Because I was with you. And because I was with you and I wanted them I started thinking maybe we shouldn't ... you and I shouldn't ... maybe I should just ... You see, that's why I went into the kitchen with what's-her-name.

**TINA:** What's-her-name?

**BOBBY:** Yeah ... What's ... her name.

*TINA gets up.*

**TINA:** You don't know her name? You don't even know her fucking name.

BOBBY: Who cares about her name. I went into the kitchen with her because I was trying to let loose, I think. I didn't care ... about you and me. I just wanted to see if I could let loose. So I—

TINA: Her name is Leah. Leeeee ... ahhhhhhh!

BOBBY: Look, don't lose it. Try to stay calm. I'm trying to explain.

TINA: Leeeee! Ahhhhh! Say it!

BOBBY: Yeah. Okay. Leah. Okay? I said it. Okay?

TINA: Sure. What else.

BOBBY: What.

*She moves really close to his face.*

TINA: Do you ... have ... something else ... to ... say ... to ... me.

BOBBY: Look, you're gonna hit me or something. I know that's what you're leading up to ... But it won't do any good because—

TINA: I'm fine. I'm not planning to do anything to you.

BOBBY: Sure you are. I know you.

TINA: Yeah? You know me. Really? Well, maybe you know me like I know you. And right now I'm thinking, I know nothing about you.

BOBBY: You know lots about me. I'm basically still me. The guy you know.

TINA: You're a child. I thought you were a man.

BOBBY: Please don't start on that child-man stuff. That just drives me nuts. I was talking to a guy at work. A guy in shipping. He's got a girlfriend who's into that child-man thing. She's always on him about it. 'Don't be a child. Be a man.' What. Did you guys all get counselling on that. Is that a thing you were taught to say. That's what the guy in shipping thinks. We were talking and—

TINA: Hey, hey. Whoa! ... I don't know where you're going with this, but it's no place useful. I wanna talk about what happened.

BOBBY: Yeah, but you started—

TINA: You got bored with the sex. That's what happened.

**BOBBY:** I never said that.

**TINA:** That's basically what you said. How could you get bored with our sex. It was ... I thought it was wonderful. Jesus it was *love* and sex. And you said it was ... well, really you never said anything except great things about it.

**BOBBY:** I was never bored. I mean I was always afraid I'd *get* bored. And I never did. But I couldn't stop being afraid that I would.

**TINA:** Yeah. Afraid. Like a child. You're a child.

**BOBBY:** (*throwing his arms in the air*) Okay, okay! I'm a child! And you're an adult! You're all grown up. I mean, come on. That's the problem. You're a hundred years old to me. You might as well be. You've just got it all figured out.

**TINA:** Oh, right.

**BOBBY:** Sure you do. Compared to me you do. You just attacked me like an adult attacks a kid. And even when you're not attacking, even when you're ... when you're loving me it's like you've got it all in place ... you've got the picture all finished and I'm just a nice part of that picture.

**TINA:** Really. You figured all this out with your friend the shipper?

**BOBBY:** No. Come on.

**TINA:** Look, just tell me what it's supposed to mean. This, I've got the picture and you're just part of the picture stuff.

**BOBBY:** Well, it makes sense of what I'm thinking now.

**TINA:** You're thinking something now?

**BOBBY:** Yeah, I'm thinking ... Listen, I gotta say this. This is what I'm thinking so I gotta say it without you hitting me.

**TINA:** Well, take your chances.

**BOBBY:** Well, I'm gonna have to, aren't I. Because what I'm thinking is important to say.

**TINA:** Really.

**BOBBY:** Yeah. Because what I'm thinking is that basically being, you know, pregnant is ... all right with you.

**TINA:** Really.

**BOBBY:** Because, well, overall it's what you wanted.

**TINA:** You saying I planned it?

**BOBBY:** No. No. I'm not saying you planned it. I'm saying you wanted it.

**TINA:** Oh. Sure. Right. So that's the story you'll tell. The little bitch was so desperate to have a kid with me she poked holes in my rubbers. Your dad will believe that no problem. He's a bigger asshole than you are.

**BOBBY:** Shit! I'm not saying that. I'm saying—well, what else do you want in life. You left school. School was nothing to you. It wasn't life. Not enough of life, anyway.

**TINA:** Well, it wasn't. It was bullshit. For me it was bullshit.

**BOBBY:** I know. For me too. Sort of. I know. But really, not like you thought it was. You knew it was bullshit because you knew there was this ... this fuck ... other thing! Yeah! This other thing. Just ... what did you call it. You had a list. You know, a simple job you liked ... and ... and—

**TINA:** A man to love. Some kids. A few good friends. A nice place to live.

**BOBBY:** Yeah. That's it. That's the list. That's Tina's list!

**TINA:** It's a good list. It's full of real things. What's wrong with it. You got a better one? Oh ... oh you do don't you. You've got a bigger better list all of a sudden. You've got dreams or something. Big ones. Is that what you're telling me. You've got *ambition* all of a sudden?

**BOBBY:** No, I've got no ambition. What's that mean.

**TINA:** Maybe you want to be a lawyer, an architect, a doctor even.

**BOBBY:** No. No, I don't. None of that's for me. I know that. All I'm saying is it's *your* list. It's what you want. And it's not just that it's what *you* want, it's that you can *say* it's what you want.

**TINA:** So say what it is *you* want. Come on. Say it. Try to say it. Maybe you can. Maybe you'll surprise us both. Maybe you're more than a dog in heat. Maybe you're a person. With a person's brain.

**BOBBY:** Ah, what's the point ...

*Pause.*

TINA:  I'm waiting. Come on, Bobby. Say something human. Show me you don't have the brain of a dog.

BOBBY:  (*sighs*) Brain of a dog. Great.

TINA:  I'm waiting. Seriously, I really am.

BOBBY:  Yeah ... Yeah, you're waiting. You're very patient. You're very understanding. You're standing there all complete or something. Everything's figured out. You've got your first kid already inside you and all you need is for me to get with it here. Just need ol' Bobby to say the right thing, put his name on a piece of paper, sign on board for the rest of his stinking life.

TINA:  Okay! That's enough. I'm history. (*starts off*)

BOBBY:  Wait a minute.

> *He grabs her.*

TINA:  Let me go.

BOBBY:  We're not finished.

TINA:  Wrong!

> *She takes a swing at him. He blocks it with his arm.*

BOBBY:  No. Screw that.

> *He grabs her.*

You're staying. We're going to—

TINA:  Look, take your hands off me, Bobby. (*struggling to get free*)

BOBBY:  No way. We've started and we're going to—

TINA:  Look, don't touch me. You've got your hands on me. I want them off—

BOBBY:  Come on, Tina.

TINA:  No! You lied to me! About everything. That's all that matters! You jerk! Everything ... anything I ever said about life or what I wanted in life you agreed with. You lying jerk! You're just weak. And ... and ... (*starts to cry*) Let me go! Let me go!

> JILL *comes running on. Yells. Drops the bag she is carrying. Rushes over. And tackles* BOBBY. *He falls. She lands on top of him.*

BOBBY:  Hey. What the hell.

JILL:  You asshole!

*They are on the ground. She is on top of him. Hitting him.* TINA *is sitting down. Crying. Pulling grass furiously.*

**BOBBY:** Come on. Stop it. Jesus!

**JILL:** You wanna beat someone up? Beat me up. Come on!

**BOBBY:** Hey. I wasn't—

**JILL:** Asshole. Coward!

**BOBBY:** Tina. Tina, get her off

**JILL:** What's wrong with you. She's pregnant.

*She is hitting him. He is trying to crawl away.*

**BOBBY:** I wasn't hurting—

**JILL:** You don't hit pregnant girls. You don't hit girls, period.

**BOBBY:** Tina! Tell her! Look. Knock it off I wasn't doing anything.

**JILL:** Yes, you were!

**BOBBY:** No, I wasn't.

**JILL:** I saw you asshole!

*Now she is standing. Kicking him as he crawls away.*

**BOBBY:** Ah. Fuck. Knock it off. Leave me alone.

**JILL:** Piece of shit.

**BOBBY:** Jesus. Ouch! Look. Leave me alone. If you don't stop I'm gonna get mad.

**JILL:** Go ahead. Get mad. I can hardly wait.

**BOBBY:** I mean it. Shit! Ouch!

**JILL:** Yeah. How's it feel! How's it feel! I said, how's it feel.

BOBBY *jumps to his feet.*

**BOBBY:** It hurts! It hurts okay?! Now knock it off or I'll rip your fuckin' face off!

*Pause.*

**JILL:** You'll what. (*approaching him slowly*)

**BOBBY:** Look. Just stay away from me.

**JILL:** You're gonna rip my face off. Is that what you said.

**BOBBY:** I ... don't want to hurt you.

JILL *is still moving toward him. He is backing up.*

**JILL:**  Do I look scared. Look at me. Do you think I'm afraid of you. Do you! (*pushes him*)

**BOBBY:**  Ah, Jesus. Okay. I give up. (*sits*) Kick me. Kick me to fucking death. Go ahead. You'll be doing me a favour. (*starts to cry*) Go ahead!

> He lies back. JILL *looks at him. Shrugs.*

**JILL:**  Piece of shit. (*goes over to* TINA) You okay, Tee?

**TINA:**  (*crying*) Great!

> JILL *sits next to* TINA. *Puts her arms around her.* BOBBY *is sobbing quite loudly now.*

**JILL:**  Hey. Shut up. You're gonna attract a crowd. Jesus. Listen to him. I've never heard a guy cry like that.

**TINA:**  Yeah … yeah. It's something, eh. He cried like that after the first time we made love.

**JILL:**  You're kidding.

**TINA:**  No. It's why I fell in love with him. (*starts to cry*)

**JILL:**  Come on, honey. He's not worth it.

**BOBBY:**  (*sits up*) I am worth it! Shit! I am worth it! I am!

**JILL:**  Shut up.

**BOBBY:**  I want an apology from you!

**JILL:**  Yeah? For what.

**BOBBY:**  Whatya mean for what. For attacking me. I didn't do anything. I wasn't hurting her.

**JILL:**  I saw you.

**BOBBY:**  You saw shit, you crazy bitch.

**JILL:**  (*leaps to her feet*) What did you call me. (*takes a step towards* BOBBY) Man, you're a glutton for punishment, aren't you.

**BOBBY:**  Tell her! Tell her, Tina. Come on!

**TINA:**  Yeah … Yeah, I just wanted to go. He was trying to stop me. That's all.

**JILL:**  He was using force.

**BOBBY:**  Come on. I just wanted her to—

**JILL:**  You had your hands on her. You were using force!

**BOBBY:**  Just a little!

**JILL:** That's too much!

**BOBBY:** But I needed her to stay.

**JILL:** But she wanted to go! If she wanted to go, she should have been able to go. And no one should have tried to stop her! Get it?!

**BOBBY:** But I ... But I ... Ah, forget it. I give up.

**JILL:** You say that but I don't think you mean it. Maybe you should though. Maybe you should just give up and crawl away. Throw yourself off a bridge.

**BOBBY:** You'd like that, wouldn't you.

**JILL:** You know I would.

**TINA:** He can't. He's got big dreams. He's got a big new life he's going to live.

**JILL:** Yeah. (*laughs*) He told you that?

**TINA:** Sure did. He's really very young, you know. But he's got a future. I mean if I don't mess it up.

**BOBBY:** I never said that.

**TINA:** And in this future are all kinds of girls and women who dress nice who he's going to do it with.

**BOBBY:** I never said that either.

**JILL:** I bet you were thinking it.

**BOBBY:** Well, I wasn't.

**TINA:** I don't know. Maybe he's been watching too much television. Maybe he's got us all confused with those kids on those shows who live near a beach. And drive nice cars. And whose parents have big houses. He's pretty ... you know ... impressionable. Did you get me a Coke?

**JILL:** Yeah.

JILL *goes looking for the bag she dropped.*

**TINA:** Is that it, Bobby. You having TV dreams?

**BOBBY:** I don't know what you're talking about.

**TINA:** Your father drives a cab. You know that, eh. You haven't forgotten.

**BOBBY:** I don't think you understood what I was saying. I think you got it wrong somehow.

**TINA:**  Maybe. Maybe not.

> JILL *hands* TINA *a can of Coke.*

Thanks ... Did you get one for him.

**JILL:**  You want him to have it?

**TINA:**  Sure.

**JILL:**  You're a saint.

> JILL *throws* BOBBY *a can of Coke. He catches it.*

Say thanks.  ·

**BOBBY:**  Thanks. I ... wanted Diet Coke.

**JILL:**  I don't buy Diet Coke. Under any circumstances. For anyone.

**BOBBY:**  I can't drink this. I might be borderline diabetic.

**JILL:**  Yeah? Drink it anyway. Find out. If you go into shock I'll get you to the hospital real fast. That's a promise.

**BOBBY:**  I bet.

> *They all pull back their tabs. Drink.* BOBBY *groans.*

**TINA:**  What's wrong. You sick?

**BOBBY:**  No ... Shit. Look at that. I almost sat on a needle. Shit.

**TINA:**  Don't touch it.

**BOBBY:**  I'm not touching it. I thought they were supposed to clean this place up. Didn't they hire people to clean this place up.

**JILL:**  No.

**BOBBY:**  I thought they were supposed to.

**JILL:**  Well, they didn't.

**BOBBY:**  Shit. It's depressing. Look at it. We can't just leave it there.

**TINA:**  Don't touch it.

**BOBBY:**  I'm not!

**TINA:**  I'll get rid of it.

**BOBBY:**  No way.

**TINA:**  Well, you're not touching it.

**BOBBY:**  Yeah well, neither are you.

**JILL:** Ah, for chrissake.

*JILL gets the bag she brought the Cokes in. Goes over. Puts it around the syringe. Picks it up. Puts it in the trash can.*

**BOBBY:** Thanks.

**JILL:** Yeah.

*They all drink.*

**TINA:** What was I saying to you, Bobby.

**BOBBY:** When.

**TINA:** Before something about something.

**BOBBY:** Something I didn't understand the point of.

**TINA:** Oh, yeah. About what your dad does for a living.

**BOBBY:** Yeah. So what? What's that got to do with anything. I mean if you're saying you can't want stuff because your parents don't have stuff, I don't get it. That's not what I was talking about before, anyway. But I still don't get it. 'Cause really I could be anything I wanted. I could go back to school and well, nothing that you needed math for but lots of other stuff. I don't know. jobs even. Just jobs better than the one I've got. Better than any job my dad ever had. I could do that.

**TINA:** So do it. Who's stopping you.

**BOBBY:** But that's not what I was saying. I'm just saying now it's wrong for you to say we can't want more because of who we are or something. What I was saying before was really ... only that I was ... young and I didn't know what I wanted ... or didn't, you know ... want.

**TINA:** Stop wanting anything. That's my advice to you. That's my advice to me too.

**BOBBY:** I'm sorry, but that's bad advice.

**TINA:** It's in the future. Wanting is tomorrow's stuff. I mean until it happens it's not real. It's not useful. Whatever it is. Ah. I can't explain it to you. You're too stupid.

**BOBBY:** No, I'm not.

**TINA:** Listen, all I'm saying ... all I wanted to say to you is ... Jesus, Bobby ... (*starts to cry a little*)

**JILL:** Don't beg him. Whatever you do don't beg.

TINA:  I just wanted to tell him one thing really. Can I just tell you one thing, Bobby.

BOBBY:  Yeah.

TINA:  Just one thing I really mean, I really believe in. Can I Bobby.

BOBBY:  Yeah ... yeah.

TINA:  Yeah. Well, it's this ... It'd be okay. You. And me. And the baby. It'd be okay. The three of us. We'd have a life. That would be ... enough. Because really there's nothing else ... better. I believe that.

BOBBY:  I know you do.

TINA:  Yeah. I know you know ... But I'm right. I believe that too.

BOBBY:  You're probably right. I don't know.

TINA:  Do you love me, Bobby ... I know you do. You weren't thinking about breaking up with me because you don't love me, were you.

BOBBY:  No. I mean ... I don't know for sure but—

TINA:  Yes, you do. You don't have to say you don't know when I know you do. I'm not that stupid. It's impossible I could be that stupid. I know when I'm loved and when I'm not loved. So just say you love me, Bobby. What's that gonna cost you.

BOBBY:  I love you.

TINA:  Do you mean it.

BOBBY:  I think I mean it.

TINA:  Jesus! Come on. You gotta mean it. What's it gonna cost you to mean it. Even if we never see each other again. You love me. We have fun. We have good sex. We have great sex, Jill. I've told you that, haven't I.

JILL:  I don't remember.

TINA:  It's true. Isn't it, Bobby. Tell her.

BOBBY:  I don't want to tell her.

JILL:  I don't want him to tell me either.

TINA:  All I'm saying is it won't get better for you, Bobby. I know that. And I know you don't know that. Your head is just full of wondering. Wondering if this. Wondering if that.

**BOBBY:** Wondering can be important. You gotta wonder.

**JILL:** Oh, for God's sake. What are you both going on about. We need decisions here. It's hard facts time. She's not going to get an abortion. We all know that. If anyone here doesn't know that he's an asshole. She's going to keep the kid. She's going to be a single mother. The only question is are you going to help her or is she going to be a single mother on welfare who lives in a rotten little basement apartment and never gets any sleep and who has a life that's basically rat shit and a future that's worse.

**TINA:** Jesus. (*starts to cry*)

**JILL:** I'm sorry. I didn't mean to upset you. I was just making a point.

**TINA:** But you could be right.

**JILL:** Nah. Really I was just making a point. But it had to be made.

**TINA:** No but ... no but ... Remember how hot it was last week. It was really hot. Anyway, one day last week about four in the afternoon, I saw a mother and her kid downtown. She was our age. And the kid was about ... I don't know ... a year. And it was asleep on her. She was waiting for a bus. I guess they'd been out, maybe to the doctor I don't know. But she looked whacked. The kid was just sprawled over her shoulder. It was sticky hot. She had a bag full of stuff she was carrying. She looked like she hadn't slept in weeks maybe. And the kid is all dead weight on her. Asleep. But holding her real tight anyway. She's just standing there like a zombie in that heat holding her kid and waiting and waiting for that fucking bus. And I knew, I just knew they were alone. There was just the two of them. And when they got home there'd still be just the two of them. Having their supper. Their bath. Going to bed. I mean I couldn't take my eyes off her and I was feeling ... well ... There was a great love. A great, great love between them. Jesus. You could just feel it. But also ... well ... sadness, eh. Sadness was in the air too. I mean I don't know if she was sad or if I was sad from watching her. Maybe she wasn't sad, maybe she was just so ... tired she wasn't feeling anything. Yeah, I don't know but maybe I was feeling all these things especially the sadness and she was just so tired she wasn't feeling anything ... Not even the love. (*gets up. Wipes herself off*) Well, that's life. Take it on the chin and ask for more. That's what my mom says.

**JILL:** Really? She says that?

**TINA:** Almost every day.

**BOBBY:** You told your mom yet? About being pregnant?

**TINA:** I thought I'd tell you first, Bobby.

**BOBBY:** Why.

**TINA:** Well, thinking about it now I haven't got a lousy clue why.

**JILL:** Maybe she thought you could tell her mom together.

**BOBBY:** Yeah ... well, we could still do that ... Are you gonna tell anyone else.

**TINA:** Yeah, I'm gonna spread it around real fast ... Is that what you're worried about.

**BOBBY:** No ... I was just asking.

**TINA:** Yeah. Right. Well, I could tell my dad. But I don't know where he is. I might track him down though. Let him know there's still guys like him in the world.

**BOBBY:** You mean me, right?

**JILL:** No, she means the fucking Pope ... Jesus.

**BOBBY:** I was ... ah, never mind. Look, I meant it when I said we could tell your mother together. Do you want to do that.

**TINA:** I don't think so.

**BOBBY:** Why not.

**TINA:** What'd be the point.

**BOBBY:** I'm the father. I know I've got responsibilities.

**JILL:** Really. What are they.

**BOBBY:** I was talking to her.

**JILL:** So now you're talking to me. Tell me what you think your 'responsibilities' are.

**BOBBY:** Being with her when she told her mom would be one. Giving her money would be another one.

**JILL:** You just heard her talk about that mother and her kid waiting for the bus and *now* you're talking about money. I just stopped hating you, Bobby. You're scaring me now. You're really terrifying me.

**BOBBY:** Yeah, right.

**JILL:** Before I thought you were just a ... guy. Just another young stupid selfish guy.

**BOBBY:** Yeah.

**JILL:** But now you're my worst nightmare. You're the worst part of all the men in the world. And you're terrifying. (*goes to the picnic table. Sits*)

**BOBBY:** (*to* TINA) What's she talking about.

**TINA:** Ask her.

**BOBBY:** No way. It's that weird thing she's got against me. And now she's got it against all the men in the world too. You think I'm gonna ask her what it is? You think I'm nuts? It's probably really rotten. I don't want to know what it is. I just want her to be nicer to me for chrissake. I'm trying to be nice here. I'm trying to do something here. I said I'd talk to your mother with you ... Okay. Wait a minute. (*walks over to* JILL) You think I didn't get upset when she talked about that young mother and her kid. You think I didn't see Tina and the ... baby ... didn't see them in my head doing that exact same thing? And living somewhere alone. I did. I saw where they lived even. It was ... shitty. They lived in a shitty place.

**TINA:** I won't live in a shitty place. No way.

**JILL:** So that's what the deal with the money was about.

**BOBBY:** Whatya mean. Sure. I guess. I couldn't let them live in a shitty place.

**JILL:** You'd save them from that, eh.

**BOBBY:** Yeah,

**TINA:** I'm not living in a shitty place.

**BOBBY:** That's what I'm saying.

**JILL:** Terrifying.

**BOBBY:** What's terrifying. How the hell is that terrifying. What the fuck are you talking about!

**JILL:**  You think it's your responsibility to save her, is that right.

**BOBBY:**  Save her from that. Yeah, I'd save her from that.

**JILL:**  You think that's your job here. That's your place in all this. You can just stand back and decide what she needs—money probably—and then throw it at her. You think you've got the final decision about where and how she lives. If she succeeds or fails. If she lives okay or she lives like rat shit. And that's terrifying! What the hell is wrong with you.

**BOBBY:**  I'm just trying to be nice!

**TINA:**  I'm not going to live in a shitty place!

**BOBBY:**  Jesus! I'm not gonna let you live in a shitty place!

**JILL:**  It's not up to you if she lives in a shitty place!

> BOBBY *starts to move around. Frantically.*

**BOBBY:**  Jesus! Christ! What?! What am I supposed to say here. Everything I say is wrong. I can't talk about money or anything. What am I supposed to do. You got something in your head for me to do? Just tell me and I'll do it! Shit! What! What?! What am I supposed to do.

**JILL:**  Fuck off and die ... You could do that.

**BOBBY:**  You first! You first! Shut up! Shut up. Fuck off. Fall down. Die. And shut up for fucking ever! What is your problem. You're driving me crazy. Don't you think I'm trying here. I've got a big thing here I'm trying to deal with. So just knock it off! Jesus. Ahh. (*starts to shake violently*) Ah shit, look at me, man. I'm outta control. (*to* JILL) Look what you're doing to me. I'm outta control here. I'm sick or something. Are you happy now.

**JILL:**  A bit.

**BOBBY:**  Shit. Look at me. Something's happening to me. And I don't even know what it is. (*to himself*) Brain of a dog ... brain of a ... dog.

**JILL:**  (*to* TINA) Brain of a what?

**TINA:**  Dog. It's something I said to him. Sit down, Bobby.

**BOBBY:**  Sit down, Bobby. Say something, Bobby. Go away, Bobby.

**TINA:**  Sit down, Bobby. Put your head between your legs. Take deep breaths.

**BOBBY:** Okay. Deep breaths. Yeah.

**TINA:** Do it. Come on.

**BOBBY:** Okay. Okay. (*whimpers, mutters to himself*) Outta control … outta control … brain of a dog, outta … control. (*drops down. Puts his head between his legs. Begins to inhale and exhale deeply*)

**JILL:** This guy's a physical wreck. Even if he did marry you he'd be dead in ten years anyway.

**TINA:** That's kind of cruel.

**JILL:** You think so? I could lay off him if you want.

**TINA:** Nah. I like the way you talk to him. Just don't make fun of his sickness. It's the one thing he can't help.

**JILL:** Sure. Whatever you say. Anything you want. I mean that.

**TINA:** You're a great friend. (*goes to* JILL. *Hugs her*) The best.

**JILL:** You too.

*They hug again.* BOBBY *is watching them.*

I'll always be there for you. Whatever you need. Ask. I'll do my best.

**TINA:** I know.

*They hug.* BOBBY *groans.*

**JILL:** What?!

**TINA:** Another needle?

**BOBBY:** No … No … that … (*groans. Gestures toward them. Groans*) I don't want to be the enemy. I mean look at you guys. You're nice to each other. Really nice. And I'm like … the hated enemy … Look, you might not believe this but I need something right now. I'm looking at you two and I'm … well, I guess what I need is *that.*

**JILL:** 'That.' What are you talking about. What's … 'that.'

**BOBBY:** That … hug. (*gestures*) Hug.

**JILL:** You need a hug.

**BOBBY:** Yeah well, I'm not totally sure. But I think I do.

**TINA:** Who from.

**BOBBY:** You … And her.

**JILL:** You need a hug from me.

**BOBBY:** Well, you're hugging her. I see what you're doing. It looks nice. I think I want it done to me. And you're here. So yeah.

**JILL:** Maybe I pushed him too far. I was just trying to shake him up. Get him in touch with reality. Maybe I've pushed him over the edge.

**BOBBY:** There's nowhere else I could go for one. My mother I guess, but ... she's so worried about my dad ... He's not well. Not that you care. I'm not even sure I care. And I don't have a friend I could ask for one. They're not that kind of guys, my friends. They'd think I'd gone you know ... gay ... They're nice guys but they don't ... touch each other.

**TINA:** Bobby, is something wrong. Are you feeling light-headed or something. It's just a hug. Why are you going on about it when our lives are falling apart here.

**JILL:** (*laughs*) No, this is good. He's talking about his tribe. Usually you can't get them to talk about their tribes. It's not allowed. All you can ever hear about them is where they go. To the mall. To the bar. To the track. So this is good. So Bobby, your tribe sounds pretty basic. Nice guys. But no hugging. You can go just about anywhere and do just about anything but you can't touch each other. If you touch another tribe member you're a pussy or a queer and you're out of the tribe. Is that basically it ... I mean they don't stomp you or anything. They don't scar your face to leave the mark of an outcast. They just say get outta here you weak little faggot or something like that.

**BOBBY:** God, man. All I was saying was it looked nice. That hug. It seemed warm and you know, cozy. Talking about tribes. Jesus. I saw the hug. I got a longing for the hug. The hug was all I was talking about, man.

**JILL:** Listen to him. He's gone nuts. His brain is soup. He's drowning in his own messed-up thoughts.

**BOBBY:** Yeah well, who's the one who was talking about tribes.

**TINA:** It's easy to hug, Bobby. You're making it sound like it's some huge magical thing beyond your powers.

**BOBBY:** That's not what I meant. I meant it was a thing about women. One of the things you can get from women that I like. The cozy thing. I'd miss that. I guess if I just slept

around I'd never really have that. You see, that's the thing.
Women offer you one or the other. The hot thing. Or the
cozy thing.

**JILL:** Ah. Now he's back on track.

**BOBBY:** But you can't have both. No way! It's not allowed. That's
a fact! You can have it hot and sexy or warm and cozy. It's a
choice.

**JILL:** Yeah, he's got a hold of his thing again. He's stroking it
good now.

**BOBBY:** No sir, you can't have both! Shit!

**TINA:** Sure you can have both.

**BOBBY:** I want to be with you, Tina! That's the truth. It is. But I
don't want to be with *just* you, Tina. That's also the truth.
Really. It's taking guts to say this, Tina. I'm trying to be a
man about this.

**JILL:** Ah, shit.

**BOBBY:** I mean I'm trying to face it. Face to … face.

**TINA:** You know your friend Nicky? That guy you play hockey
with.

**BOBBY:** What about him.

**TINA:** Every time I see him I get wet.

**JILL:** Bingo! Bullseye! Ding! A thousand points! (*laughs*)

**BOBBY:** (*to* TINA) You get what.

**TINA:** In my pants. Wet. And hot.

**BOBBY:** Holy fuck.

**TINA:** Really wet and hot.

**BOBBY:** Holy fuck! Don't say that. What are you doing. You
don't have to talk like that.

**TINA:** It's a chemistry thing. Sometimes he looks at me and I
can't breathe.

**BOBBY:** Jesus, you're gonna keep talking about it.

**TINA:** I mean the guy, there's just something about him. He
looks at me. My nipples get hard.

**BOBBY:** (*sort of writhing. Covering his ears*) I'm not listening to this
shit. No way.

TINA:  He looks at me and I go home and think about him. I try
not to. I'm guilty at first because he's your friend. He's your
left winger. But then I think, what's the harm, I'm just
thinking. So you know I just think it all the way through. In
my head, I mean. In my head I get him in my bedroom. Take
off his clothes.

BOBBY:  Ah Jesus, Tina. Come on.

JILL:  Keep going, girl.

TINA:  I gotta keep going. I'm getting excited just talking about
him. No way I can stop now.

BOBBY:  Jesus.

TINA:  I get him naked. He's got a great ass. He's really, you
know ... what's the word.

JILL:  (*shrugs*) Big?

TINA:  Really big.

JILL:  Really big?

TINA:  The biggest.

BOBBY:  Oh, yeah. Right. Gotta be the biggest. Great. Well, who
cares. I'm not small you know. I know that. I'm okay about
that. I may have the brain of a dog, but I don't have, you
know, the dick of a dog.

TINA:  Oh, be quiet.

JILL:  That brain of a dog comment made a real impression, eh.

BOBBY:  I'm just saying if you're doing a number on me you
can't do it on the dick.

TINA:  Knock it off! This isn't about you and your dick. It's about
me.

JILL:  It's about you and Nicky's dick.

TINA:  Right. So where was I. In my head, I mean.

JILL:  In your head he's naked. In mine too.

TINA:  Yeah?

JILL:  So keep going.

TINA:  So I get naked too. I take off my clothes real slow. And
while I'm doing it, he gets hard. I want to hold it. It looks

powerful. It's a powerful hard thing he's got. He's gotta put it somewhere. I'm wondering where should I let him put it first.

**BOBBY:** Come on! Come on! Okay, okay okay okay. I get it. Okay? I get the number you're doing. You don't have to make this shit up. You don't think things like that.

**TINA:** Listen. I'm being honest about this. It's taking guts but it's only fair I tell you 'cause you told me.

**BOBBY:** But you made it up!

**TINA:** Wrong! Your friend Nicky turns me on. And I could name three other guys we both know who turn me on. And once every few weeks or so I see some guy on the street who turns me on. And that's the facts! And now we both know the facts!

*BOBBY puts his head between his legs.*

**JILL:** Hey, Bob. You wanna hug?

**BOBBY:** I'm gonna puke.

**TINA:** (*shrugs. Looks at* JILL) I guess he really didn't know.

**JILL:** Never entered his head.

**TINA:** Hard to believe … Come on, Bobby. Didn't it ever occur to you that maybe I could feel the same way you do about that stuff—

**BOBBY:** No.

**TINA:** Never?

**BOBBY:** No.

**TINA:** Well, now that you know, how do you feel.

**BOBBY:** I told you. I wanna puke.

**JILL:** Ah, grow up.

**TINA:** Yeah, she's right. Throw up. Then grow up.

**BOBBY:** Come on. How would you feel if I told you I wanted to do it with Jill.

**TINA:** Do you.

**BOBBY:** No.

**TINA:** Then I'd wonder why you were lying.

**BOBBY:** Suppose I really did want to.

**TINA:** Do you.

**BOBBY:** No!

**TINA:** Then what's the point!

**BOBBY:** You don't get it.

**TINA:** No, you don't get it. I'm trying to deal with real things here. Real feelings. If you've got any real feelings we can talk about them. If you want to screw Jill we'll deal with it. If you want to become a lawyer we'll work out a way you can do that. If you want to be a father to our baby we'll make that happen. But if you think you're the only one in serious confusion here, if you think you're the only one who wants more than one thing, maybe a few things that don't go together, we're not going anywhere useful with this. You might as well just go home.

**BOBBY:** I don't want to go home.

**TINA:** No? Are you sure.

**BOBBY:** Pretty sure.

**TINA:** So what *do* you want to do. Do you have any idea what you want to do.

**BOBBY:** When.

**TINA:** Now.

**BOBBY:** No.

**TINA:** But you don't wanna go home.

**BOBBY:** No.

**TINA:** Do you want us to leave you here alone.

**BOBBY:** I don't know.

**TINA:** Do you wanna keep talking.

**BOBBY:** I don't know.

**TINA:** Do you wanna have sex with Jill. Do you wanna think about having sex with Leee-ahhh! Do you wanna puke. Do you wanna tell me why you don't care if your dad's sick. Do you wanna tell me what you want to do with your life, you know just give me a little hint. Do you wanna know what *I'm* gonna do. Do you, Bobby. Do you wanna know even just a little what I'm gonna do.

**BOBBY:** Yeah. I do.

**TINA:** I'm going to have this baby.

**BOBBY:** I knew that.

**TINA:** Take some time off from the store. Have the baby. Get my mom to help out a bit. Go back to work. Bring up the baby. Hang out with my friends when I get the chance. That's about it.

**JILL:** You left out having great sex.

**TINA:** Yeah. Have some great sex, when I can, with whoever.

**JILL:** Great guys. Maybe older guys.

**TINA:** Whoever

**BOBBY:** Nicky, probably.

**JILL & TINA:** Ah, grow up!

> BOBBY *gets up. Brushes himself off.*

**TINA:** You going somewhere?

**BOBBY:** No.

**TINA:** You look like you wanna go.

**BOBBY:** Yeah. Well

**TINA:** Go ahead.

**BOBBY:** I'm not really sure what I—

**TINA:** Look Bobby, you might as well go away. What are you gonna tell me if you stay. I've pretty much got the picture. All you can do now is lie. You can say you wanna marry me or something. And what an enormous stinking lie that'd be. I mean I guess you've come through this. We put a lot of pressure on you here. I was willing to do anything to keep you. Really I was. But I've come through that. I don't feel that way anymore. I don't know why. But you can go. You can go that way. (*points*) And I'll go that other way. And we don't have to see each other ever again. You can send money if you want. Or not. I don't care.

**JILL:** I do. Your mom will too.

**TINA:** She's right. But I want you to know when you're in court for non-payment it won't be my idea. Because *we* were special to me. And anything less than special is shit. Pressure's off. Go home. Go on.

> *Pause.*

**BOBBY:** Is this a trick.

TINA:  No. Go. It'll be all right.

BOBBY:  What'll be all right.

TINA:  Everything. Don't worry. You can just leave ... See ya.
Take care of yourself.

> JILL *walks to* BOBBY. *Puts out her hand.*

JILL:  No hard feelings.

> BOBBY *just looks at her hand.*

Come on. Put it there.

> BOBBY *looks at them both.*

BOBBY:  What's goin' on.

TINA:  Nothing. It's over.

BOBBY:  What's over.

TINA:  Everything. You and me. Just forget it.

BOBBY:  Forget what.

TINA:  Everything.

> JILL *puts out her hand.*

JILL:  No hard feelings.

BOBBY:  What the hell is it with you people. Whatya mean, it's
over. Just like that, it's supposed to be over. You're fucking
me around.

TINA:  No, I'm not.

JILL:  She means it. I mean it too.

BOBBY:  What. What do you mean.

JILL:  No hard feelings. It's over between us too.

BOBBY:  What's over. What's between us to be over.

JILL:  My lifelong hatred and disappointment in you. Fifteen
years of bad feelings. You're out of her life. Means you're out
of mine finally. Why hold a grudge. Come on. Shake. I'd feel
better if you did.

BOBBY:  Really. Talk about weird shit. I'm supposed to shake
your hand to end some weird rotten thing we've had since
kindergarten that I never even understood. And then you're
just gonna walk out of here with your friend who just
happens to be carrying my baby inside her and that's the

end of that. You're fucking me around. Aren't you. Aren't you fucking me around. And if you are, why. Why do this to me. I'm willing to reach an agreement here. That's really all I've been trying to do, you know. Reach an agreement. I never wanted an abortion. I never said I wanted an abortion so that must mean something.

**TINA:** It means nothing. If I wanted an abortion. I'd get one. I wouldn't care what you thought about it.

**BOBBY:** You wouldn't?

**TINA:** Why should I.

**BOBBY:** I don't know. But I guess ... well, I wasn't saying you should anyway. I was just trying to say something ... right. Saying I'd agree to whatever you want, whatever you say ... to just, you know, be there in some way. I never said I wouldn't be there for you, in some way, Tina. I never said that. So why are you doing this. Why are you saying it's over. It's like you're giving up.

**TINA:** I told you. It was special. Now it's shit.

**BOBBY:** I don't think it's shit. It might not be as special as it was but it's definitely not shit.

**JILL:** Come on. Shake. Be a man!

**BOBBY:** Put your fucking hand down. Stay away from me. Stop messing with me. Look, I know you're smarter than me. You always were. You go to university.

**JILL:** Community college actually.

**BOBBY:** The point is you're smarter than me.

**JILL:** But who isn't.

**BOBBY:** I just want you to stop messing with me. I'm just trying to be nice here.

**TINA:** Nice doesn't cut it. Nice is shit. I wanted you to be brave and strong and grown up. I need someone strong and grown up.

**BOBBY:** I'm trying to grow up. I wanted to grow up. That was always what I was aiming for. I didn't know I had to do it all of a sudden. I was hoping I'd get some time.

**TINA:** You were braver when I first met you. You're weaker now. And younger too. I think you're going in the wrong direction.

**JILL:** I think that too. If she keeps you around by the time the kid is born she'll be changing diapers for both of you.

**BOBBY:** Look. I told you to shut up.

**JILL:** Did you. When was that. I must have missed it. Tell me again. Come over here. And tell me. Come real close.

**BOBBY:** This is a good thing for you, isn't it, Jill. This has gotta be the high point of your life so far, I bet. Getting to give me the gears. You're a sick person. That's what I think. I'm gonna stop wondering why you've been so rotten to me. I'm gonna stop wondering what's so rotten about me that's made you treat me like garbage and I'm gonna start thinking you did it just because you're mean and sick.

**JILL:** Hey, didn't I offer my hand to you. Didn't I offer you the chance to make up, you asshole. All you had to do was leave.

**BOBBY:** I'm not leaving. You leave.

**JILL:** I'll leave when she leaves.

**BOBBY:** Well, she's not leaving and neither am I.

**TINA:** I think you should leave, Bobby.

**BOBBY:** I'm not going anywhere!

**TINA:** But it's over.

**BOBBY:** Don't say it's over.

**TINA:** But it is.

**BOBBY:** You don't mean that.

**TINA:** Yes, I do.

**BOBBY:** How. How can you mean that. That's cold. That's so fucking cold. You're doing this like you're just closing a door or something. Something simple like closing a door. There, click it's closed. That simple. How can you get so cold, so fast. That's just ... mean. Yeah, it's mean. Don't be mean, Tina. I never was mean to you. Okay, I was selfish and I fucked around a bit. But I wasn't mean. Don't be mean, please. I hate it.

**TINA:** I'm sorry. I'm not trying to be mean. I'm just being practical. You're not going to be any help to me. I can't see you being a useful part of my life, that's all.

**BOBBY:** You're just saying that now. Because of how I am now. But how I am now isn't necessarily me. I mean I'm under pressure and—

**TINA:** You handled the pressure okay. You protected yourself okay. You didn't commit yourself to anything here. You told me about the things you needed. The time. You told me about your dreams.

**BOBBY:** Ah, don't start with the dream stuff. I never said anything about dreams. That was you.

**TINA:** No. It was you. It was all about you. You you you.

**BOBBY:** Ah, Jesus. That's just how it sounded. Come on. I was under attack.

**TINA:** No, that's just how it sounded. I gave you opportunity. You could have said some stuff. You could have gone forward. Made a move. Got involved in the possibilities.

**BOBBY:** What. You saying it was a test or something.

**TINA:** I didn't mean it to be a test. But maybe it was. Maybe it was a test.

**BOBBY:** Yeah. And I failed. Well, no surprise there. Now that you put it that way I get it. Just another failure. Just someone else to let down. Okay. I can live with that. That's no big deal. I've been doing that all my life.

**JILL:** Ah, Jesus. (*to* TINA) You've opened up something pretty ugly here. We're not gonna have any fun with this at all. He's just gonna—

**BOBBY:** Hey, it's just the truth, okay. I'm sorry if it's not entertaining enough for you. All I'm saying is the stinking truth. I'm a failure. Ask my dad, he'll tell you. Ask my foreman at work. But ask him fast because I probably won't last there very long. Ask any of the teachers I had. (*points to* TINA) Ask her mother. Her mother's not gonna be surprised I let her down. I know she expected it. I've felt her expecting disappointment from me ever since I met her. Ah, fuck it. It's just life. Who cares. I don't know. Maybe I didn't take it seriously enough. Or maybe I wasn't good enough to have a

life in the first place. Yeah, maybe I'm good enough to live
but not good enough to have a life worth living. Now that's
confusing. Where's my jacket. Did I bring anything else. Ah,
who cares. Okay, I'm outta here. Good luck. Good luck to
you, Tina. I give up. So what's new, eh. (*starts off muttering*) I
give up. What's new about that. You thought it was sex and
good times, Bobby. Well wrong! Okay, live and learn. Live
and learn. What. Learn what. I don't know. Grow up. (*stops*)
Yeah. Grow up, asshole ... Stupid little asshole.

> BOBBY *is just standing there. Head lowered. Muttering to himself*
> '*stupid little asshole*' *over and over again.* JILL *and* TINA *are watching*
> *him. Occasionally looking at each other. This goes on for a while.*
>
> *Suddenly a siren goes by on the street. And then another. And another.*
> *Pause.*

I ... think I'll go see what's going on ... It ah ... sounded like
they were headed the way I was goin' anyway.

> *He shrugs. He leaves.* JILL *and* TINA *watch him silently. He is gone.*
> TINA *looks at* JILL. JILL *shrugs.*

JILL:  I guess he just needed a graceful way out.

> TINA *starts to wander around, gesturing.*

You okay?

TINA:  What.

JILL:  You okay?

TINA:  I don't know.

> *Pause.*

JILL:  I'm just glad he didn't get into any detail about his father. I
bet that would have been truly ugly. You know, ugly in that
boy man son dad boy dad dad son boy boy kind of way.

TINA:  Yeah ... His dad ... You ever meet his dad?

JILL:  No. Thank you, God.

TINA:  An asshole.

JILL:  And his mom?

TINA:  Wife of an asshole ... She tries but ... Well, what can she
do ...

JILL:  He drinks, right?

**TINA:** Drinks. Messes around. Spends a lot of time with his buddies ... But mostly he drinks. Bobby never drank. There was that about him.

**JILL:** Yeah, there was.

**TINA:** I mean he couldn't anyway. Because of his condition.

**JILL:** Yeah. It's pretty pathetic that he used being drunk as an excuse for messing around. I mean he knew you knew he couldn't drink.

**TINA:** He was desperate. At first, I thought it was good he was desperate. Because maybe being desperate meant he really wanted to keep me ... Wrong again! It's just the way he is. Desperate. But for what. What's he want. He's gotta want something. What is it!

**JILL:** Maybe after what he's been through here, he just wants to go home and put his head in a vice. Get some guy in his tribe to tighten it for him.

**TINA:** We were pretty hard on him I guess.

**JILL:** You think so?

**TINA:** I don't know. Maybe.

**JILL:** You weren't. You were just trying to get to the bottom of something. I was hard on him. But that's only because I hate all men. (*laughs*)

**TINA:** (*sits*) Do you.

**JILL:** Come on.

**TINA:** No. Really. Do you hate them all. I'd understand if you did.

JILL *walks over to* TINA.

**JILL:** But I don't ... Well ...

**TINA:** Sometimes?

**JILL:** Yeah, sometimes. But ... sometimes ... other times ... you can be with one of them and it seems okay ... Some guy, an ordinary guy. He talks to me like I'm a human being. He seems like one himself. And I think, this is good. This is all we need. To like each other. I think, hey yeah, I like this guy. A lot. Kind of ... Well, at least he doesn't want to kill me or maim me. So I guess ... some of them I like. A few. This doesn't happen often. I've only met a few I like. Two actually. But I'm still young. (*sits next to* TINA)

TINA: I can't see myself being with anyone for a long time. Being close to any guy. Talking ... or anything. It's all outta the question ... because I'm ... you know ...

JILL: Yeah, you're pregnant.

TINA: Really.

JILL: Yeah.

TINA: Pregnant with Bobby's child ... But ... he's gone. So I'm, you know ...

JILL: You're not alone.

TINA: No. I'm not alone. But I'm pregnant with someone's child ... who isn't here. Someone who's gone. I mean the father's gone. So that's different ... There's a different feeling about the whole thing now.

JILL: What is it.

TINA: I don't know yet. I mean he just left ... It'll take some time to understand it.

JILL: He was never really involved. He was never a sure bet.

TINA: I had hopes. I loved him, you know. I still love him.

JILL: Yeah ... Why.

TINA: You mean why still.

JILL: No. I guess I meant why ever.

TINA: Reasons ... You know you might fall in love sometime with some guy I hate. And the reasons will be ... I mean why you love him and I hate him ... Well, we'll never know, maybe.

JILL: I hated Bobby because I never saw him show any concern for anyone or anything besides himself.

TINA: I loved Bobby because he cried when we made love. And because ... Well, because I thought he loved me.

JILL: Well, now we know.

TINA: I mean more or less that's why.

JILL: Well, we know more or less.

　　　*Pause.*

TINA: God. I *am* young. Really. Think about how young I am.

JILL: That's not necessarily a bad thing ... You mean you're scared?

TINA: I'm not giving up this baby. No way am I giving up this baby.

JILL: I know that.

TINA: I mean not even a little. My mom's not gonna raise it or anything. I mean she can help ... But she's gonna be the grandmother. I'm the mother. There's not gonna be any confusion about that. Not like Grace what's-her-name.

JILL: Gallagher.

TINA: Yeah ... Her mother's raising that kid. Her mother's the mother really. Grace is just doin' the stuff she did before. Hanging out with her friends. She goes to bars. Just like nothing happened. What kind of crap is that. That's bullshit. Don't you think that's bullshit.

JILL: Well, I don't know what their circumstances are. I mean knowing Grace it's probably better for the kid.

TINA: I'm not gonna do it that way.

JILL: Well, you're not Grace Gallagher.

TINA: No way am I Grace Gallagher. Not even a little. Not even one little stinking piece of my brain is like her. You ever hear anyone saying we're the same, you gotta straighten them out.

JILL: I will.

TINA: Because, Jesus, well, the only thing that's the same is ... well, you know ...

JILL: What.

TINA: Well, who's the father of Grace's kid.

JILL: Beats me.

TINA: Yeah. That's my point. He's gone. So it's the same. The father thing for my kid is gonna be the same as it is for Grace Gallagher's.

JILL: That's not necessarily bad.

**TINA:** Except it gives me something in common with her, and she's a total fucking idiot ... and ... also it's different. Different than the way I thought it would be ... A bit harder. A lot harder probably.

> *Pause.*

**JILL:** So you're really giving up on him? Bobby.

**TINA:** Yeah ... Well, what's the point ... I mean I've got to make plans. I've got to be real about this thing. It's my life. I've got to get it off on the right foot. There can't be any confusion about this. I mean look around this world we live in. All you see is confused people fucking up. And they're fucking up because they're confused about where they stand ... about ... just about everything really ... So you can't have basic stuff like who wants each other and who wants this kid just floating in the air. That's bullshit.

**JILL:** Yeah ... I just meant he might go away and think about it.

**TINA:** He'll miss me. I know. He'll come sniffing around. He'll make it hard and confusing. I'm gonna have to convince him to just leave me alone ... My mom went through this with my dad. My dad sniffed around for a long time. My mom waited for us to come together as a family. Until I was five or six. She tried. Maybe he even tried too. But it finally just fucked up ... I'm not going down that road. I gave Bobby his chance.

**JILL:** Yeah.

**TINA:** Yeah.

> *Pause.*

**JILL:** Yeah. But ...

**TINA:** What.

**JILL:** Maybe not. I'm just thinking now. About guys our age. Maybe we should talk about this some other time. I mean—

**TINA:** No, go ahead. Come on.

**JILL:** Well you're never gonna meet a guy your age who's got as much figured out as you do. Well, a few ... Maybe ...

**TINA:** But not Bobby.

**JILL:** Fucking 'A' not Bobby. Look, I'm gonna try and be fair here. Forget my personal feelings about him for a while. I mean I can't stand the little prick. And I really loved kicking him. I really did. But maybe we should be looking down the road here. Considering all the possibilities ... you know, you being alone with the baby and still having these feelings for Bobby, and finding some way to make him understand that he—

TINA: I told you. I can't do that. It's gotta be up to him. And it's gotta be clear.

JILL: Yeah. But you see, the thing about most guys is ... It's true someone's gotta kick them when they're acting like a crazy dog. But what I'm saying is after you kick them maybe you gotta give their adolescent brains a chance to focus in on what's happened. 'Hey, I've been kicked like a crazy dog. I wonder why. Gee.' ... Okay. That's hard. That sounds hard ... Ah shit it, why don't they just get it ... Why are we always made to feel bad for trying to get them to act like just basic human fucking beings! Sometimes I get the feeling they wanna suck my brains out and tie me naked to the nearest tree and fuck me to death. Because that's what they think I'm for. That's my purpose. To give them pleasure. Even if it kills me! Okay okay, I got that out of my system. So what I'm thinking, I've thought this for a while, is maybe they just need more time and instruction. Time and instruction through those dangerous stupid years between about fourteen and twenty-six. Maybe it's that simple. Maybe we have to help them. Maybe that's part of our purpose here on earth. Not all of it. Not all of it by any shot. But part of it ... So?

TINA: I've got a kid due in about eight months. If you want to become some kind of tutor for Bobby that's up to you.

JILL: I was thinking of conditioning. You know, lock him in a room. Then show him a thousand pictures of people in situations where they don't get to do what they want to do. No one gets to do what they want to do in any picture. They only get to do what they have to do. You know, like an adult.

TINA: How about love.

JILL: I think adult love is better. Okay. It's not ... pure or anything. It's mixed up with lots of other things. Responsibility. Guilt even. But overall it's better. It's got a chance of lasting. So?

TINA: What.

JILL: You wanna work on Bobby a little more? Turn him into an adult human being?

TINA: No.

JILL: Why not. It might be fun.

TINA: No. He's gotta do it on his own. For his own reasons. I mean *really* he does ... I gotta eat something.

JILL: Okay ... What.

TINA: Anything.

JILL: You getting sick yet? You know, in the mornings.

TINA: I don't want to talk about that. It comes later anyway. You got any money?

JILL: Hey. You're the one with the job. I'm a starving student.

TINA: But I'm pregnant. I'm a single-mother-to-be. I'm headed for a life of despair and shiftiness.

*They start off.*

JILL: Over my dead body.

TINA: Mine too. Not that I wouldn't take welfare if I had to.

JILL: Why the hell shouldn't you if you had to.

TINA: And I'd try not to be ashamed.

JILL: Why the hell should you be ashamed. It's there. The money's there. And if it's not there, it should be there. What other great things are they doing with it. I mean have they got better things to do with it than give it to mothers ... If you ever have to take welfare and if anyone ever makes you feel ashamed for taking it, you tell me and I'll kick them to death.

TINA: It's a deal ... And also if you hear people talking about me that other way, you know, feeling sorry for me and making me sound all sad and pitiful ... kick them to death too. Will you do that.

JILL: Definitely.

BOBBY *comes on.*

BOBBY: Hey!

*They turn toward him.*

So ... You leaving?

**TINA:** Yeah.

**BOBBY:** Yeah ... So ... I came back.

**TINA:** Yeah ...

**BOBBY:** You see, I've ... It's just that ... well, I've been ... I've been thinking ...

**TINA:** Good for you. Keep it up.

TINA *walks past* JILL, *and leaves.*

**JILL:** She means that.

JILL *winks. Turns and leaves.* BOBBY *watches them. Pause.*

**BOBBY:** Hey! ... Hey, I ah ... I ah ... (*to himself*) Hey. Hey ...

BOBBY *sits down. Gestures a couple of times. Shrugs. Scratches his ear.*

*Blackout.*

*End.*